"It is always important to evaluate a book, at least partially, in terms of who it is written for. Welty's book is written for (a) people who have heard of Plantinga's contributions, but do not quite understand them or what makes them significant, (b) people who have heard that Plantinga is a Calvinist philosopher, but do not know what that means or how he qualifies, and (c) people who have heard that Plantinga's contributions are controversial amongst pastors, theologians, and others whom they trust. Has Welty succeeded in writing a book for these three audiences? Yes, there is no doubt that he has hit his targets. But he has actually succeeded in writing a book for an additional audience, namely, academic philosophers. Persons who devote their careers to understanding this stuff will also greatly benefit from Welty's contribution. His succinct summaries of Plantinga's major contributions, his valuable insights into Plantinga's Christian philosophical method, and his analysis of Plantinga's relationship to the Reformed tradition make this book worthwhile for academics as well as any Christian interested in seeing how Athens and Jerusalem relate. I had a hard time putting it down and looked forward to picking it back up."

—**David E. Alexander**, Associate Professor of Philosophy, Academic Dean, Providence Christian College

"Alvin Plantinga is one of the titans of contemporary Christian philosophy, and it would be almost unforgivable to omit him from P&R's Great Thinkers series. His writings over the course of a six-decade career combine an astonishing degree of creativity with rigorous analytical precision, a delightful sense of humor, and a refreshingly uncomplicated Christian piety. Until now, there has existed no reliable introduction to Plantinga's work that I could enthusiastically recommend to students, pastors, and other interested readers. That deficiency is now remedied with the publication of Greg Welty's *Alvin Plantinga,* a superlative addition to an already excellent series. As a seasoned teacher-scholar with advanced degrees in theology and philosophy and a firm commitment to confessional Reformed doctrine, Dr. Welty was the ideal person to write this book. In a concise and eminently readable style, he clearly explains Plantinga's major contributions and argues that, despite his deviations from the Reformed tradition at points, his most valuable contributions can be comfortably accommodated by that tradition. I would never suggest reading only one book on Plantinga, but if it must be one, make it this one."

—**James N. Anderson**, Carl W. McMurray Professor of Theology and Philosophy, Reformed Theological Seminary, Charlotte

"Alvin Plantinga is arguably the greatest philosopher of religion the world has seen during the past one hundred years. A book summarizing his views and assessing them from the Reformed perspective is, therefore, a very apt contribution to the Great Thinkers series at P&R Publishing. In this delightful little volume, Greg Welty has done a masterful job of selecting pertinent positions from Plantinga's formidable corpus, explicating them accurately and accessibly for readers unfamiliar with his work, and evaluating them fairly in light of the Reformed heritage."

—**Michael Bergmann**, Professor of Philosophy, Purdue University

"Alvin Plantinga is arguably the most brilliant Christian philosopher of the modern era. His work has profound implications for theology, apologetics, and a Christian worldview. Greg Welty has done us a tremendous service by carefully canvassing the life and work of Plantinga, who has never been easy to categorize within the spectrum of Christian thinkers. Plantinga was reared in the Dutch Reformed tradition, and much of that influence comes through in his work. Welty helpfully demonstrates the contributions that Plantinga makes, specifically to Reformed thinking as it touches on his work in the areas of faith and reason, the problem of evil, theistic arguments for God's existence, the attributes of God, and the relationship between Christianity and science, to name a few. Plantinga has set himself on the leading edge of nearly all these topics, and if the thinking Christian is going to grapple with their implications for the faith, then they need to be familiar with Plantinga's arguments. I can't think of a better place to be introduced to those arguments than Greg Welty's excellent and very accessible little volume."

—**Scott Christensen**, Associate Pastor, Kerrville Bible Church, Kerrville, Texas; author, *What about Free Will?* and *What about Evil?*

"Even a nonphilosopher like me knows how important Alvin Plantinga is. But he's also prolific: how can I get a sense of his contributions and also of appropriate critiques? In this work, Greg Welty offers—in a friendly, approachable, and trustworthy manner—both a sympathetic survey of Plantinga's distinctives and a fair-minded evaluation of them (no mean feat!). I come away thankful for Al Plantinga, grateful to Dr. Welty for such an achievement, and strengthened in my own Christian confidence."

—**C. John ("Jack") Collins**, Professor of Old Testament, Covenant Theological Seminary

"Alvin Plantinga is undoubtedly one of the most important philosophers of the last several decades. And he is among the most important *Christian* philosophers ever. Unfortunately, most Christians outside academia know little about him, and many in Reformed circles who are familiar with him are wary of his ideas. Fortunately, Greg Welty's book makes Plantinga's contribution to philosophy and the defense of Christianity accessible to the wider Christian community and illumines his enduring relevance both to Christian thought generally and to the Reformed faith in particular. I wish I could put a copy in the hands of every pastor and church leader!"

—**Steven B. Cowan**, Chair, Department of Humanities, Professor of Philosophy and Religion, Lincoln Memorial University

"Greg Welty has done both the philosophical and the Reformed communities a tremendous service with this book. In short compass, he provides an impeccably clear and reliable guide to Plantinga's thought to which any philosopher might profitably turn, and also a helpful, critical analysis of it from an orthodox Reformed standpoint. Anyone reading this book should come away, not just with a better understanding of the content and merits of Plantinga's work, but also with a deeper understanding of the many philosophical and theological issues that it raises."

—**Daniel Hill**, Senior Lecturer in Philosophy, University of Liverpool, UK

"Alvin Plantinga has obviously contributed a great deal to the Christian defense of theism and supernatural faith. At the same time, apologetic gains are sometimes made at the expense of theological essentials. This book, by a highly competent philosopher, weighs both of these influences in careful analysis. I recommend this survey highly to anyone who wants to defend classical (including Reformed) theism in the current philosophical climate."

—**Michael Horton**, J. Gresham Machen Professor of Systematic Theology and Apologetics, Westminster Seminary California

"Dr. Welty has masterfully presented the highlights of Alvin Plantinga's thought. Clear, concise, and accessible, this will be the first book I recommend to anyone interested in Plantinga's epistemology, especially as Plantinga's project relates to Reformed theology. I am glad Plantinga was included in the Great Thinkers series, and I am equally glad that Dr. Welty agreed to take on this project."

—**Scott Oliphint**, Professor of Apologetics and Systematic Theology, Westminster Theological Seminary

"Welty brings theological sophistication as well as philosophical expertise to this project. He clearly and authoritatively explains the central themes and ideas in Alvin Plantinga's formidable philosophical project, and goes on to offer some key points of criticism from a Reformed perspective. This is the perfect resource for anyone who wants an accurate and accessible introduction to Plantinga's work and its significance."

—**Jerry L. Walls**, Professor of Philosophy, Scholar in Residence, Houston Baptist University

"I applaud P&R for publishing this volume in the Great Thinkers series, and I applaud Greg Welty for writing it. There is no living Christian philosopher who has been more influential than Alvin Plantinga, and anyone who wants to understand how Christian philosophy in particular has evolved during the last sixty years simply must be acquainted with Plantinga's work. In this little volume, Greg Welty superbly introduces the philosopher and his work. His treatment of Plantinga's contributions in epistemology, philosophical theology, and philosophy of religion more generally are fair, insightful, and highly accessible. Both those who are and those who are not yet acquainted with Plantinga's work will find in Welty an exceptionally capable and clear guide. Even Reformed philosophers (like me) who are steeped in and greatly influenced by Plantinga's work will find this book a delightful and thought-provoking read. Especially valuable are Welty's critical assessments of Plantinga's thought about genuinely Christian philosophy and the relationship of his work to the Reformed tradition. I hope and pray that our Lord will use this fine introduction to inspire more Reformed thinkers to become Christian philosophers."

—**John Wingard Jr.**, Professor of Philosophy, Department Chair, Dean of Humanities, Covenant College

Alvin

PLANTINGA

GREAT THINKERS

A Series

Series Editor
Nathan D. Shannon

Available in the Great Thinkers Series

Thomas Aquinas, by K. Scott Oliphint
Francis Bacon, by David C. Innes
Karl Barth, by Shao Kai Tseng
Richard Dawkins, by Ransom Poythress
Gilles Deleuze, by Christopher Watkin
Jacques Derrida, by Christopher Watkin
Michel Foucault, by Christopher Watkin
G. W. F. Hegel, by Shao Kai Tseng
David Hume, by James N. Anderson
Immanuel Kant, by Shao Kai Tseng
Karl Marx, by William D. Dennison
Alvin Plantinga, by Greg Welty
Karl Rahner, by Camden M. Bucey

Forthcoming

Plato, by David Talcott
Adam Smith, by Jan van Vliet

Alvin

PLANTINGA

Greg Welty

P.O. BOX 817 • PHILLIPSBURG • NEW JERSEY 08865-0817

ISBN: 978-1-62995-853-8 (pbk)
ISBN: 978-1-62995-854-5 (ePub)

Printed in the United States of America

Library of Congress Cataloging-in-Publication Data has been applied for and is available with the Library of Congress.

To my sons

James, Nathan, and Jeremy

CONTENTS

SERIES INTRODUCTION

Amid the rise and fall of nations and civilizations, the influence of a few great minds has been profound. Some of these remain relatively obscure even as their thought shapes our world; others have become household names. As we engage our cultural and social contexts as ambassadors and witnesses for Christ, we must identify and test against the Word those thinkers who have so singularly formed the present age.

The Great Thinkers series is designed to meet the need for critically assessing the seminal thoughts of these thinkers. Great Thinkers hosts a colorful roster of authors analyzing primary source material against a background of historical contextual issues, and providing rich theological assessment and response from a Reformed perspective.

Each author was invited to meet a threefold goal, so that each Great Thinkers volume is, first, *academically informed*. The brevity of Great Thinkers volumes sets a premium on each author's command of the subject matter and on the secondary discussions that have shaped each thinker's influence. Our authors identify the most influential features of their thinkers' work and address them with precision and insight. Second, the series maintains a high standard of *biblical and theological faithfulness*. Each volume stands on an epistemic commitment to "the whole counsel of God" (Acts 20:27), and is thereby equipped for fruitful critical engagement. Finally, Great Thinkers texts are *accessible*, not burdened with jargon or unnecessarily difficult vocabulary. The goal is to inform and equip the reader as effectively as possible through clear writing, relevant analysis, and incisive, constructive critique. My hope is that this series will distinguish itself by striking with biblical faithfulness and the riches of the Reformed tradition at the central nerves of culture, cultural history, and intellectual heritage.

Bryce Craig, president of P&R Publishing, deserves hearty thanks for his initiative and encouragement in setting the series in motion and seeing it through. Many thanks as well to P&R's director of academic development, John Hughes, who has assumed, with cool efficiency, nearly every role on the production side of each volume. The Rev. Mark Moser carried much of the burden in the initial design of the series, acquisitions, and editing of the first several volumes. And the expert participation of Amanda Martin, P&R's editorial director, was essential at every turn. I have long admired P&R Publishing's commitment, steadfast now for over eighty-five years, to publishing excellent books promoting biblical understanding and cultural awareness, especially in the area of Christian apologetics. Sincere thanks to P&R, to these fine brothers and sisters, and to several others not mentioned here for the opportunity to serve as editor of the Great Thinkers series.

Nathan D. Shannon
Seoul, Korea

FOREWORD

Alvin Plantinga has been the most influential Christian philosopher over the last half century. Prior to meeting him in 1987, I had only a dim notion of who he was and no idea how much he had already done to open the world of professional philosophy for sincere—even Reformed—followers of Jesus Christ. First as his student and fellow worshiper, and then as a teaching assistant and appreciative colleague, I have come to know Alvin Plantinga as a brother in Christ and a model of Christian philosophical boldness. Even though I have followed Plantinga's career carefully and, through him, have come to know many of the Christian philosophers mentioned in this book (Nicholas Wolterstorff, William Alston, and Richard Swinburne, among others), Greg Welty has written a better introduction to Plantinga than I could have written. Although I find Plantinga easy to read (in part because I can hear his twinkle-in-the-eye Dutch voice), his arguments are often philosophically subtle. Welty explains these arguments with uncommon clarity. More than that, Welty systematizes Plantinga's body of work more successfully than any other account I have seen. In this brief foreword, I hope to show that Alvin Plantinga is a sincere believer who knows Jesus personally, that he is at the heart of the revival of Christians being taken seriously in the world of professional philosophy, and that his service to Christ's kingdom is most evident in the army of professional academics emboldened to overtly integrate their faith with their academic work, even in the midst of an academic world hostile to Christ's lordship.

Out of a desire to impress my pastor, I started reading Francis Schaeffer when I was in middle school and resolved to major in philosophy in college. At Covenant College, I took five courses with Gordon H. Clark; then I studied under John Frame and about Cornelius Van Til at Westminster Seminary in California. Before I started my PhD work at the University of Notre Dame, Schaeffer, Clark, Van Til, and Frame were what "Christian philosophy" meant to me. I still greatly value their insights and influence, but they were Christian philosophers called to speak to fellow Christians about the world of philosophy. At Notre Dame, I met Christians called to speak to fellow philosophers about Christian beliefs. Alvin Plantinga was the boldest of all these Christian philosophers. I took two graduate courses from Plantinga: "Ontological Issues" and "How to Be a Christian Philosopher." The title of the second course was exotic (and nonstandard), but it was descriptive. The course counted as epistemology, but the readings and discussion revolved around deciding whether a follower of Jesus should be an "Augustinian" or a "Thomist" in philosophical method. In chapter 7, Welty explains where Plantinga lands on this question, and it is on the side of boldness: unashamedly using what we know from Scripture to identify philosophical problems worth solving and to give us premises to use in solving those problems.

In the spring of 1990, Plantinga asked me to be his teaching assistant for a course he would teach at Calvin College one night a week. Every Wednesday for fifteen weeks, I would ride with him in his old van from South Bend, Indiana, to Grand Rapids, Michigan. We would talk philosophy during the two-and-a-half-hour drive, arriving in time to join his father (Cornelius) and younger brother (Neal, not yet the president of Calvin Seminary) for dinner. The conversation was about ideas, almost always ideas close to what Alvin Plantinga calls "the great things of the gospel." We would talk about philosophy and Christian doctrine all the way home after he taught his class. I graded the student exams and essays for the course. I doubt any of those students learned more than I did from the experience.

Alvin Plantinga and his wife sat in front of my wife and me in the worship services at the South Bend Christian Reformed Church for the five years I was studying at Notre Dame. I have been examining people for church membership for the last seven years as a ruling elder in a PCA church, and I teach through Jonathan Edwards's *A Treatise concerning Religious Affections* at Reformed Theological Seminary. Based on Alvin Plantinga's profession, life, and work, I am convinced that his faith in Christ is deep and genuine. He knows he is a sinner, whose only hope is the blood of Jesus Christ, and his aim is to serve Jesus with all his ability. Over the thirty-five years I have known him, he has grown in the fruit of the Spirit. He is a faithful husband and loving father; he is a man of prayer. When he writes about what faith feels like from the inside (that it is nothing like a leap in the dark), he is reporting his own experience. When he insists that he *knows* that Jesus rose on the third day because the Holy Spirit revealed it to his mind and sealed it to his heart on reading it in the Word of God, he is describing what happens to him as he reads Luke 24. Hearing anyone express their faith in this way is thrilling. What is distinctive about Plantinga's profession is his audience: the world of professional philosophy.

By "the world of professional philosophy" I mean the community of people paid to teach and "do" philosophy: people with PhDs in philosophy, with full-time positions at colleges or universities, especially schools with graduate programs in philosophy. Plantinga's audience is this world. When he entered this world in the 1950s, it already had the characteristics of what Charles Taylor calls "secularism-3" in *A Secular Age*: it was obvious to everyone in that world that there is no spiritual reality and that only ignorant people take religion seriously. It would have been easy (and worldly-wise) for Plantinga to keep his Christian convictions to himself and focus his research on the questions that already seemed important to his peers and professors. He didn't. Welty's brief description of Plantinga's education highlights his discovery, as a student, that the arguments against what he believed about God were weak. Exposing the weakness of anti-theistic arguments remained a lifelong passion for Plantinga. The audience he wanted to convince was the world of professional philosophers. Although I have not heard Plantinga refer to his work as a calling, it seems evident to me that he was called to defend the Christian faith to the world of professional philosophers.

In his closing chapter, Welty rightly asks why so much of Plantinga's career has been spent defending (mere) theism. The question is apt, since Plantinga repeatedly exhorts Christian philosophers to defend the full range of Christian beliefs, and not merely the existence of God or the coherence of the idea of God. Welty correctly notes that Plantinga's work in *Warranted Christian Belief* and "O Felix Culpa" defends specifically Christian beliefs, and that these are significant accomplishments. It seems likely, though, that Plantinga gives so much attention to defending theism because the world of professional philosophy struggles to get past objections to theism. His primary audience is that world, so their questions set the agenda for his work. He wants other Christian philosophers to use their philosophical training to serve other communities, and especially to serve the church. I keep up with about two dozen of Plantinga's former graduate students at Notre Dame. We all have the experience of being encouraged in our work for the church by Alvin Plantinga.

The impact that Plantinga has had on the tiny world of professional philosophy over the last fifty years is admitted by everyone in that world. In 1991, I carried his briefcase (literally) when he defended his *Warrant and Proper Function* at an "author meets critics" session at a meeting of the American Philosophical Society. ("Author meets critics" sessions are by invitation only and are, in practice, the highest honor that the APA extends. Only the most influential philosophers in the world each year are invited, and three "critics" prepare essays that they read during the first part of the session. The rest of the time is spent by the author responding to the critics and then taking questions from the floor.) The room was packed. Nearly thirty of the philosophers present in the room had authored views that Plantinga had rejected in *Warrant: The Current Debate*, the book that preceded *Warrant and Proper Function.* This was their first opportunity to take him on in public. The importance of his work was recognized by all, and before long the focus of the discussion was whether one could embrace his model of warrant (as proper function) without also acknowledging the existence of a Designer of our cognitive equipment. In a room full of people dismissive of Christian beliefs about God, Plantinga took this question seriously. He allowed that one could try to believe in design without a Designer, but he said that it would be hard to do so. He had no trouble believing in *and worshiping* the Designer, and he suggested that they would find epistemology less frustrating if they did, too.

Commending belief in a Designer is not evangelism. When the audience consists of over one hundred anti-theist philosophers, though, it isn't chopped liver. No altar call was issued, but the audience's inability to find holes in either Plantinga's model of warrant or the epistemological advantages of having a divine Designer in the model made it hard for his critics to dismiss Christian convictions. Maybe just as important was the effect that Plantinga's boldness had on the Christian philosophers in the room (and those they told about the event). It is possible to read Plantinga's entire corpus and conclude that while he is clearly very good at what philosophers do, he doesn't do much that goes beyond what can be found in Edwards or Bavinck. From a theologically Reformed perspective—as Welty deftly discusses in chapter 8—Plantinga's work sometimes strays from Reformed convictions. Plantinga is not Berkhof, but it is not his aim to be Berkhof. It is to be a Christian defending and commending Christian belief to other philosophers. Plantinga is very, very good at this task.

What makes Plantinga a thinker worthy of including in a series with Hume, Marx, Derrida, and others is the (now) hundreds of Christian academics who have been inspired by his exhortations and example to use their talents, training, and time to serve the church and to deploy what they know from Scripture in their work. Plantinga worked with a handful of brave believers to form the Society of Christian Philosophers in 1978. It is now the largest philosophical society in the world. Even though Plantinga never offers a complete theory of apologetics (and never takes systematic positions on the possibility of neutral common ground, the role of presuppositions, or the use of evidences), nearly all of his work *does* apologetics: he gives reasons for the hope he has in Christ, answers objections to Christian belief, exposes the futility of non-Christian belief systems, and comforts believers who doubt. The Christians who studied philosophy under him, heard him at conferences, or read his books typically were emboldened to speak more openly about their faith and to focus their work on problems that would meet needs outside merely academic discussions. Beyond the narrow world of professional philosophy, Plantinga's approach to Christian scholarship in general now figures prominently in the philosophy of education statements at numerous Christian colleges and universities. Plantinga's "Christian philosophical method," which Welty explains so well in chapter 7, is easily generalized to all academic disciplines. I know this because for the last fifteen years I have been the coordinator of faculty development at Covenant College. I have used Plantinga's approach to Christian scholarship as a guide to the integration of Reformed Christianity with all the disciplines at Covenant. Christian scholars with PhDs in psychology, English literature, education, and biology (to name only a few) have deepened and extended the role of their faith in their work, working off of Plantinga's approach.

Plantinga is a "great thinker" because of his impact. I cannot end this foreword, though, without emphasizing what a fine job Greg Welty has done in this volume. His writing is clear, carefully organized, and philosophically precise. His summaries of Plantinga's arguments show a serious command of both Plantinga's texts and the issues involved. Welty is concise without being pedantic. He uses direct quotations from Plantinga's works in a way that allows Plantinga to speak for himself. His critique of Plantinga in chapter 8 asks the questions most likely to be of interest or concern to thoughtful Reformed readers, and his analysis is charitable, even when it is expressing misgivings. This volume is a reliable guide to Plantinga's work. I will be making it required reading for my undergraduate philosophy students.

Bill Davis, PhD
Professor of Philosophy
Covenant College
Adjunct Professor of Systematic Theology
Reformed Theological Seminary

PREFACE

This book draws upon nearly twenty years of teaching Alvin Plantinga's philosophy in the seminary classroom at the master's and doctoral levels. While he is only one of many philosophers to whom I expose my students, I think he is one of the "greats," not only in religious philosophy, but also in philosophy more generally (for reasons you will soon discover). My goal in teaching philosophy is to make the subject accessible, while helping students do four things: cultivate intellectual skills that are useful for Christian life and ministry, acquire intellectual insight into the relationship between one's theological conclusions and philosophical precommitments, encounter the rich heritage of Christian contributions to philosophy, and begin preparing a Christian defense against the wide range of criticisms that have become influential in our day. Philosophy is a hard subject, but it is also an extremely useful subject; evangelicals only hurt themselves and others when they pretend otherwise on either count.

I first heard of Plantinga in 1991 as a philosophy major at UCLA, when my history of philosophy professor, Art Flemming, happened to make an offhand comment during office hours. He commented that "the Reformed epistemologists like Plantinga were doing good work." "Who is that?" I wondered, and a follow-up in the campus library led me to *Faith and Rationality* (1983), edited by Plantinga and Nicholas Wolterstorff. I was stunned by the rich series of reflections in this book (as well as in Wolterstorff's *Reason within the Bounds of Religion*). I had been a Christian for five years, since my conversion in high school, but I had never heard of these thinkers. Then in 1992, as a student in Robert Adams's Introduction to Philosophy of Religion course at UCLA, there were brief references in his lectures to Plantinga's material on the ontological argument. Adams himself was a major contributor to the contemporary revival of this medieval argument for the existence of God, but through him I became acquainted with Plantinga's contributions as well.

Later, as a student at Westminster Seminary (California), I was introduced to John Frame's comparison of Plantinga and Cornelius Van Til, largely through "Appendix I: The New Reformed Epistemology," in Frame's *The Doctrine of the Knowledge of God* (the main text for his Christian Mind course). In his Modern Apologetics course, Frame also assigned Geivett and Sweetman's *Contemporary Perspectives on Religious Epistemology*, which included a whole section on Reformed epistemology. My interest in Plantinga's contributions was thereby sustained, though he certainly wasn't central to the Westminster curriculum.

It was during my MPhil and DPhil years at Oxford that my awareness of Plantinga's work became deeper, more comprehensive, and even life-changing. I had hitherto been dazzled by Plantinga's gift for seemingly defeating his opponents with one hand tied behind his back: he presented an author's position more strongly than the author himself had presented it, only to demolish it anyway. And his whole presentation was seasoned with a zany sense of humor, so what's not to like? I was happy to have such a spokesman for the Christian faith in "my" corner. But my supervisor, Richard Swinburne, seemed to be on the opposite side of Plantinga in many philosophical debates, and, in my naïveté, this was bewildering to me. Swinburne was an internalist in epistemology, but Plantinga was an externalist. He thought that probabilistic, cumulative-case natural theology worked, but Plantinga had severe doubts. He thought that God's ignorance of the future was vast, but Plantinga defended a traditional view of divine omniscience. He thought that recent, "skeptical theist" approaches to the problem of evil were useless, but Plantinga thought they were profoundly insightful. He didn't think that God existed in all possible worlds, but Plantinga did. He thought that Molinism didn't work, but Plantinga accepted, developed, and applied Molinist claims. (If these concepts strike you as strange and unfamiliar, then you're in the right place. The rest of this book will explain these terms.)

Here were arguably the two most influential Christian philosophers of the second half of the twentieth century; how could they be split down the middle like this? And then it dawned on me: I had been instinctively accepting many of Plantinga's positions, taking them for granted, perhaps because he (like me) was an American, and by the late 1990s he had become quite famous in American philosophy-of-religion circles. I simply gave him the benefit of the doubt on a first reading and didn't ask too many questions. He seemed convincing! But the Brits were having none of it. Nothing about Plantinga was taken for granted; you had to fight for every inch of territory. I encountered countless British philosophy students (and some dons) who didn't care how many people thought Plantinga was a good philosopher. What was the *argument*? Was it any good? Why should we take his starting points as ours? Allegedly, he had his head in the Platonic clouds—advocating "possible worlds" and "creaturely essences"—while the sensible British were doing more down-to-earth "ordinary language philosophy."

This conflict was very good for me. It taught me to be, well, a philosopher—not only to be aware of multiple views held by equally capable individuals, but also to consider deeply who had the better argument, and to be less superficial in figuring this out. It's natural to be attracted to, and to want to find, thinkers who reinforce our current beliefs, but that is not enough. All sides should be heard and considered thoughtfully, insofar as we are able to do so. Our conversation partners—people made in the image of God whom we want to both influence and learn from—deserve at least that. Swinburne assigned Plantinga's works for several of my tutorial essays, alongside lots of other works, and though I did end up taking Plantinga's side several times, I had to defend that in oral argument. This led to a more valuable and enduring appreciation of his contributions, for many of his positions (though not all!) stood the test, as far as I could tell. That appreciation informed my dissertation, has informed my teaching career since then, and informs this book. Perhaps in starting the journey of carefully examining Plantinga's work and that of others, you also will be led to be a philosopher!

The chapters to come will introduce you to Plantinga's thought on faith and reason, the problem of evil, arguments for the existence of God, the divine attributes, religion and science, and Christian philosophical method. I apologize in advance for not covering his considerable and substantive work in metaphysics and in philosophy of mind. For a short book, I had to make compromises, and these latter two areas didn't seem as relevant to the focus of the book. Believe me, this felt like cutting off my own arm, since my dissertation substantively draws upon many of Plantinga's insights into possible worlds metaphysics.

In closing, I'd like to thank James Anderson (at RTS Charlotte) and Daniel Hill (at the University of Liverpool) for reading through an earlier version of this manuscript and offering some clarifying comments.

ABBREVIATIONS

Works by Plantinga

AdvCP	"Advice to Christian Philosophers"
AEAAN	"An Evolutionary Argument against Naturalism"
ANat	"Against Naturalism"
AugCP	"Augustinian Christian Philosophy"
AW	"Afterword"
AWalls	"Ad Walls"
CLPL	"A Christian Life Partly Lived"
CPE20C	"Christian Philosophy at the End of the 20th Century"
DGHAN	*Does God Have a Nature?*
EAAN	"The Evolutionary Argument against Naturalism"
EPAE	"Epistemic Probability and Evil"
GAFE	"God, arguments for the existence of"
GFE	*God, Freedom, and Evil*
GOM	*God and Other Minds*
IBIGR	"Is Belief in God Rational?"
KCB	*Knowledge and Christian Belief*

LCO	"Law, Cause, and Occasionalism"
MICP	"Method in Christian Philosophy: A Reply"
NatT	"Natural Theology"
NN	*The Nature of Necessity*
OCS	"On Christian Scholarship"
ORTCA	"On Rejecting the Theory of Common Ancestry: A Reply to Hasker"
OWO	"On Ockham's Way Out"
PAFE	"The Probabilistic Argument from Evil"
PFNT	"The Prospects for Natural Theology"
RBG	"Reason and Belief in God"
SOFC	"Supralapsarianism, or 'O Felix Culpa'"
SP	"Self-Profile"
SS	"The Sceptics' Strategy"
TDOSTA	"Two Dozen (or so) Theistic Arguments"
TFWD	"The Free Will Defense"
TOCA	"Truth, Omniscience, and Cantorian Arguments: An Exchange"
WCB	*Warranted Christian Belief*
WCD	*Warrant: The Current Debate*
WPF	*Warrant and Proper Function*
WTCRL	*Where the Conflict Really Lies*

1

WHY ANOTHER BOOK ON PLANTINGA?

Is Plantinga One of the Greats?

The Great Thinkers series includes volumes on luminaries of unquestioned and unrivalled influence: Thomas Aquinas, Francis Bacon, David Hume, Immanuel Kant, G. W. F. Hegel, Karl Marx, Jacques Derrida, and Richard Dawkins. Why include a volume on late twentieth-century (and early twenty-first-century) Christian philosopher Alvin Plantinga? Does he have a right to join this grand gathering?

If we were to ask Plantinga himself, he might say, "Maybe not!" In his own words, his is "a Christian life partly lived." As of this writing, he has not yet completed his task on earth. Besides,

> my spiritual life and its history isn't striking or of general interest: no dramatic conversions, no spiritual heroism, no internal life of great depth and power, not much spiritual sophistication or subtlety, little grasp of the various depths and nuances and shading and peculiar unexplored corners of the spiritual life.

> It is very much an ordinary meat-and-potatoes kind of life. (CLPL, 45)[1]

But thankfully, this isn't a series on great lives, but rather on great *thinkers*. Dispassionate observers of history know that only time will tell whether Plantinga should be classed with any of these "greats." But for the time being, it is obvious that he is a prime candidate to be so labeled by future generations. There is good reason to think he *will* be categorized with other twentieth-century intellectual writers of great religious influence, such as Bertrand Russell, Ludwig Wittgenstein, C. S. Lewis, Karl Barth, Cornelius Van Til, and Richard Swinburne, who through their careful arguments and power of expression molded the thought of many in their generation and beyond.

In short, a volume like this is needed because of the quantity and quality of Plantinga's philosophical work on behalf of Christian theism and because of the influence he continues to have to this day.

Plantinga's Significance

Measured Quantitatively

Plantinga's significance can be measured quantitatively in at least two ways: his amount of writing and the number of different topics addressed. On average, Plantinga has published three peer-reviewed articles every year for nearly six decades and written or edited fourteen books during that time. This astonishing pace of written work has generated an even greater amount of further philosophical discussion by others. Between 1985 and 2021, at least twenty-two substantive and scholarly books were published

1. All references to Plantinga's work use the abbreviations found on the previous "Abbreviations" page. Full bibliographic information for every work cited can be found under "References" at the end of the book.

about Plantinga's philosophy, and there are hundreds of articles and doctoral dissertations arguing about his work. To give just three examples: the author of *Thomas Aquinas* in this series did his doctoral dissertation at Westminster Theological Seminary on the apologetical implications of Plantinga's epistemology, the author of *David Hume* did his doctoral dissertation at the University of Edinburgh applying Plantinga's epistemology to paradoxical theological beliefs, and my own dissertation at Oxford developed an argument for the existence of God from an unpublished but widely circulated lecture by Plantinga. And that's just staying close to home by surveying P&R writers within this series!

In addition to the sheer quantity of his writing, the topics Plantinga has addressed range over a majority of the subdisciplines of philosophy: metaphysics, epistemology, philosophy of religion, philosophical theology, natural theology, philosophy of science, and philosophy of mind. Not only is such a cross-disciplinary capability rare, but some of these writings are among the most widely anthologized and reprinted pieces on the philosophy of religion in the past forty years, including "The Free Will Defense," "The Reformed Objection to Natural Theology," and "On Ockham's Way Out." Uncommon indeed is a book of readings in religious philosophy published nowadays without including something Plantinga wrote. For better or for worse, his work has become canonical.

Measured Qualitatively

Even more importantly, Plantinga's significance can be measured qualitatively against that of other Christian philosophers. First, while writing in a largely secular and even anti-theist milieu of professional philosophy, Plantinga has utilized and developed distinctively Christian sources. He has done so as a means of addressing important philosophical questions that have been debated for millennia. This includes drawing upon Augustine on free will theodicy, Boethius on philosophy of language, Anselm on the ontological argument for God's existence, Aquinas on the natural knowledge of God, Ockham on the nature of foreknowledge, Luther on the nature of faith, Calvin on the *sensus divinitatis* and on the Holy Spirit's production of Christian faith, Molina on free will and providence, Jonathan Edwards on religious affections, perception of God, and religious belief, and Herman Bavinck on properly basic belief in God. (True to his Dutch Reformed heritage, there is also appeal to the Belgic Confession on trust in Scripture being produced by the Holy Spirit and to the Heidelberg Catechism on the nature of faith.)

While we can question whether Christian orthodoxy is compatible with *every* theme that Plantinga utilizes from Augustine, Boethius, Anselm, Aquinas, Ockham, Luther, Calvin, Molina, Edwards, and Bavinck, there is no debate that these are all distinctively Christian theologians. For a philosopher to come to prominence in the 1960s and continue dialoguing with a wide array of his peers to the present day by regularly and robustly drawing upon insights from the full range of the Christian tradition is rare indeed.

Second, it is hard to overestimate Plantinga's influence on contemporary discussion and philosophical practice. Prior to Plantinga, sightings of past Christian thinkers were relatively rare in philosophy journals (outside of specifically Roman Catholic scholarship). Now they are commonplace, particularly in philosophy of religion, but increasingly in epistemology, metaphysics, and even philosophy of science. By no means is this cultural transition in Anglo-American philosophy the result of Plantinga's work alone. (The contributions of Richard Swinburne, Robert and Marilyn Adams, William Alston, Nicholas Wolterstorff, and Paul Helm come to mind.) But without Plantinga's pioneering work, this change would have been significantly less likely.

Third, Plantinga's work is self-consciously characterized by a bold methodological stance. With a doggedness that sometimes irritates his detractors, he insists that there is nothing inappropriate, unseemly, or embarrassing for a Christian philosopher to simply start with and then use Christian assumptions in his academic work, despite the widespread rejection of these assumptions by the majority of modern thinkers. One does not need lengthy prolegomena that argue for the right to bring one's religious convictions to the table. Rather, one simply announces that this is the starting point and proceeds accordingly. Fairly early in his career, in the inaugural issue of the now flourishing philosophy journal *Faith and Philosophy*, Plantinga published a clarion call for more Christian philosophers to do this (an essay to which we will return in chapter 7). Plantinga's steadfast refusal to do philosophy in a "religiously neutral" way is due to his Dutch Reformed upbringing, as we will now see.

Plantinga's Personal Background

Upbringing

In 1985 Plantinga published a 95-page intellectual autobiography called "Self-Profile" (SP) for a volume dedicated to his academic contributions. The first third of this contains quite a bit of information about his upbringing, academic training, and teaching career. In 1993 he revised and somewhat expanded this material in "A Christian Life Partly Lived" (CLPL).

Plantinga was born in 1932 to Cornelius and Lettie Plantinga in Ann Arbor, Michigan. His father and mother both traced their ancestry to the Netherlands. His grandparents on both sides were raised in churches of "the *Gereformeerde Kerken,* dedicated to the practice of historic Calvinism" (SP, 4). Alvin Plantinga strongly agrees with the view of these churches "that education is essentially religious; there is such a thing as *secular* education but no such thing as an education that is both reasonably full-orbed and *religiously neutral*" (SP, 4). He favorably mentions "the leadership of the great theologian and statesman Abraham Kuyper (premier of the Netherlands from 1901 to 1905)" and his role in establishing "a Calvinist University in Amsterdam: the Free University" (SP, 4).

Plantinga recalls that in his childhood church, "many had read their Kuyper and Bavinck, and a few were considerably better at theology than some of the ministers in charge of the church" (SP, 6). After marrying Lettie while a student at Calvin College, Plantinga's father became a graduate student in philosophy at the University of Michigan, then got his PhD in philosophy at Duke University, and then taught at Huron College, a Presbyterian college in South Dakota. Because his father later moved on to teach at Jamestown College, Plantinga's formative junior and senior high school years were spent in North Dakota. He decided at the age of fourteen that he wanted to become a philosopher, partly because of his father's life and teaching. His influence was firmly embedded in a larger church context:

> We attended the Presbyterian church in Jamestown; but I heard about as many sermons from my father as from the minister of the church we belonged to. He often preached in churches in nearby villages that were without a minister, and I often accompanied him. I went to church, Sunday school, a weekly catechism class my father organized, and weekly "Young People's" meetings. I also remember a series of mid-week Lenten services that were deeply moving and were for me a source of spiritual awakening. (CLPL, 49)

Education (1953–58)

BA from Calvin College (1953). Plantinga started his college studies at Jamestown College (where his father taught), but after just one term he transferred to Calvin College in Grand Rapids, Michigan, because his father had become a psychology professor there. He then spent a semester at Harvard University—on a scholarship he applied for "just for the fun of it"!—but returned to Calvin permanently after attending some classes there taught by William Harry Jellema, "the most gifted teacher of philosophy I have ever encountered" (SP, 9). Nicholas Wolterstorff, who would also go on to become an influential Christian philosopher, was one of Plantinga's classmates at Calvin, and they both took Jellema's courses.[2] Plantinga received his BA from Calvin College in 1953. He had three majors (philosophy, psychology, and English literature), and took six courses in psychology from his father.

Plantinga shares a deep conviction that was instilled in him by his education at Calvin:

> Christianity is indeed profoundly relevant to the whole of the intellectual life including the various sciences. . . . Serious intellectual work and religious allegiance, I believe, are inevitably intertwined. There is no such thing as religiously neutral intellectual endeavor—or rather there is no such thing as serious, substantial and relatively complete intellectual endeavor that is religiously neutral. (SP, 13)

Plantinga's teachers at Calvin, including Jellema, thought that "the history of philosophy was at bottom an arena in which conflicting religious visions compete for human allegiance. Philosophy, as they saw it, was a matter of the greatest moment; for what it involved is both a struggle for men's souls and a fundamental expression of basic religious perspectives" (SP, 13).

After we survey Plantinga's contributions to philosophy in the next five chapters, we will see in chapter seven that the foundation Plantinga received at Calvin exerted an incalculable influence over his intellectual outlook and methodology, despite that outlook being immediately put to the test by a secular

2. About thirty years earlier, the famous Christian apologist Cornelius Van Til had also taken Jellema's classes. Van Til graduated from Calvin College in 1922.

graduate school environment largely inhospitable to orthodox Christianity. Plantinga describes the magnitude of his decision to stay as an undergraduate at Calvin after flirting with Harvard:

> I found Jellema deeply impressive—so impressive that I decided then and there to leave Harvard, return to Calvin and study philosophy with him. That was as important a decision, and as good a decision, as I've ever made. Calvin College has been for me an enormously powerful spiritual influence and in some ways the center and focus of my intellectual life. Had I not returned to Calvin from Harvard, I doubt (humanly speaking, anyway) that I would have remained a Christian at all; certainly Christianity or theism would not have been the focal point of my adult intellectual life. (CLPL, 53)

Calvin College bequeathed an equally momentous blessing: it was there that Plantinga met Kathleen De Boer, a fellow Calvin undergrad, whom he would marry in 1955 while pursuing his graduate studies. "Her family, like mine, was of Dutch Christian Reformed immigrant stock" (SP, 14). They have four children—Carl, Jane, William Harry, and Ann—who

> are for us a source of enormous joy and satisfaction. . . . I also loved (and love) the children with a passion, and did spend a lot of time caring for them; and I immensely enjoyed playing, talking, arguing, wrestling, singing, hiking and just being with them. Our dinnertimes were often a kind of rich but wacky discussion of ideas ranging over theology, philosophy, psychology, physics, mathematics, literature and what dumb thing someone's teacher had said today. (Since all of our children took courses from me at Calvin, the teacher in question was sometimes me.) (CLPL, 59, 278 fn. 8)

Plantinga's "life-long love affair with mountains" also started during this period, when he traveled to the West Coast for the first time in 1954 to visit his fiancée's hometown in Washington. "Splendidly beautiful, mysterious, awe-inspiring, tinged with peril and more than a hint of malevolent menace—I had never seen anything to compare with them" (SP, 14). Mountaineering and rock-climbing have been an important part of Plantinga's life ever since, and his favorite climbs repeatedly appear as illustrations in his philosophical writing. They also trigger his *sensus divinitatis* ("sense of the divine"), a topic we will explore in the next chapter.

MA from the University of Michigan (1955). After finishing at Calvin, Plantinga started graduate work in philosophy at the University of Michigan in January 1954, studying under William P. Alston, Richard Cartwright, and William K. Frankena (SP, 16). (Nelson Pike, who would write a seminal article on the human free will / divine foreknowledge dilemma, and pen an important early book on divine timelessness, was a fellow student with Plantinga in Alston's courses.)

Plantinga received his MA in philosophy from Michigan in 1955. There he was exposed to anti-theist arguments in a hostile environment, and he consequently

> developed a lasting interest in the sorts of attacks mounted against traditional theism—the claim that it was incompatible with the existence of evil, the Freudian claim that it arose out of wish fulfillment, the positivistic claim that talk about God was literally meaningless, the Bultmannian claim that traditional belief in God was an outmoded relic of a pre-scientific age, and the like. All but the first of these, I thought, were totally question begging if taken as arguments against theism. (SP, 18)

The fact that Plantinga found these arguments so weak did not keep him from writing quite a bit about them in his future work, probably because he saw it as important to get the word out that they *were* weak, despite their popularity.

Plantinga found his teachers clear and thoughtful, and his "time at Michigan was pleasant and instructive." But "I yearned for something more; philosophy there, it seemed to me, was too piecemeal and too remote from the big questions. I missed the insight and illumination conveyed by Jellema's lectures. The fare at Michigan, I thought, was a bit too sere [i.e., dry or withered] and minute" (SP, 19).

PhD from Yale University (1958). According to a Michigan professor whom Plantinga consulted, at Yale University "philosophy was done in the grand style of the German idealists" (SP, 19). So Plantinga left to pursue his PhD studies there in 1955, rather than continuing at Michigan after his MA. But while Yale was much bigger and more diverse in terms of students and faculty, Plantinga's "main complaint [was] that there was scarcely any opportunity to learn how to do what philosophers do. . . . No one seemed prepared to show a neophyte philosopher how to go about the subject—what to *do*, how to think about a problem to some effect. Fundamentally, it was that high level of generality that was at fault" (SP, 20).

In addition, Plantinga was greatly bothered by the "attitude of irony and distance" (SP, 21) towards philosophy among many Yale students and some faculty. This mindset encouraged merely becoming conversant with the extant answers to philosophical questions, rather than discerning the truth. Whereas Plantinga felt that philosophy at Michigan failed to aim at the big questions, at Yale it failed to seek the right answers. Both contrasted sharply with the expectations for philosophical discourse generated at Calvin when he was an undergraduate. This concern was not alleviated in his final year at Yale, even though he was teaching in its Directed Studies program. He now had "a job at Yale and reasonable prospects for permanence," but his frustrations over "metaphysics in the Grand Style, at least as practiced at Yale" (SP, 22), led him to accept Wayne State University's vigorous efforts to recruit him as a professor.

Teaching Career (1958–2010)

Wayne State University (1958–63). While the beginning of Plantinga's teaching career was technically that final year at Yale, in fall 1958 he was hired to teach philosophy full time at Wayne State University in Detroit. "It was one of the best decisions I ever made . . . perhaps the best thing that has happened to me" (SP, 22). His colleagues included Hector Castañeda, Edmund Gettier, Richard Cartwright, and Keith Lehrer, with whom Plantinga developed extraordinary camaraderie. Their

> philosophy department was less a philosophy department than a loosely organized but extremely intense discussion society. . . . We discussed philosophy constantly, occasionally taking a bit of time to teach our classes. . . . What impressed me most about my new colleagues was that they seemed to have a way of *doing* philosophy. There wasn't nearly as much talk *about* philosophy—what various philosophers or philosophical traditions said—and a lot more attempts actually to figure things out. (SP, 23)

Their joint efforts at collective philosophical criticism gave Plantinga five years of invaluable practical training, which he would apply with great success in his future years, having finally received a vision of how to *do* philosophy:

> I remain enormously grateful for those days at Wayne and I continue to have the most profound respect for the members of that early group. It was from them and in company with them that I learned how philosophy ought to be approached;

> it was in company with them that I learned the importance of genuine clarity and rigor in the subject, and something of how to achieve them. (SP, 28)

Calvin College (1963–82). Despite his wonderfully "stimulating and educational" experience at Wayne State, Plantinga accepted an offer to start teaching at Calvin College in fall 1963, replacing his retiring and much-admired undergraduate mentor, Harry Jellema. Plantinga's decision to leave for Calvin involved "considerable agony." Nevertheless, it was

> eminently sensible. I had been an enthusiastic Christian since childhood and an enthusiastic Reformed Christian since college days. I endorsed the Calvinist contention that neither scholarship nor education is religiously neutral; I therefore believed it important that there be Christian colleges and universities. I wanted to contribute to that enterprise and Calvin seemed an excellent place to do so. (SP, 30)

In particular, Plantinga wanted to work on

> the connection between the Christian faith and philosophy (as well as the other disciplines) and the question how best to be a Christian in philosophy. Calvin was the best place I knew to work on these questions; nowhere else, so far as I knew, were they as central a focus of interest and nowhere else were they pursued with the same persistent tenacity. I therefore went to Calvin. (SP, 30)

Over the next nineteen years, Plantinga found the vibrant Christian philosophical community he sought. Two things characterized his years as a professor at Calvin. "First, in the philosophy department there has been just the sort of communal effort at

Christian scholarship I was hoping to find" (SP, 30–31). A faculty colloquium met "nearly every Tuesday for the last eighteen years . . . to discuss and criticize each other's work" (SP, 31). Plantinga wrote or edited seven books and wrote forty-seven articles during the Calvin years, and much of this material was discussed with fellow faculty members. Second, another "attractive feature of academic life at Calvin—as, perhaps, at any medium sized college—is the opportunity to make friends in other disciplines" (SP, 32). These included significant friendships with scientists, historians, and mathematicians, as he brushed up on topics that intersected with his own research interests.

University of Notre Dame (1982—2010). It seems inconceivable that after nineteen years at Calvin College, Plantinga would willingly leave that fruitful and spiritually rewarding intellectual environment. But when he briefly visited other institutions during the Calvin years, he discerned that he was most successful as a teacher when instructing graduate students, and "Calvin has no graduate students." In addition, there was beginning to emerge at the University of Notre Dame the largest "concentration of orthodox or conservative Protestant graduate students in philosophy . . . in the United States." Leaving Calvin for Notre Dame would enable him "to take part in the building of a graduate department of philosophy that is both first rate and Christian." And so that is what he did in 1982, despite finding "the prospect of leaving Calvin disturbing and in fact genuinely painful" (SP, 33).

Plantinga has not written a lot of material about his twenty-eight years teaching philosophy to graduate students at the University of Notre Dame. Sharing in church community, hearing good preaching, and participating in Sunday school continued to be quite important to him personally (CLPL, 67–68). Perhaps what impressed him most during this period was the great difficulty in making real progress on the question of how to be a Christian philosopher, rather than just being a Christian who does philosophy. It is one thing to *want* to be a Christian philosopher, and to want to be successful at it. It is quite another to figure out what that entails. The heart of his answer, which he continued to work on quite deeply and systematically during the Notre Dame years, is that "following Augustine (and Abraham Kuyper, Herman Dooyeweerd, Harry Jellema and many others), I believe that there is indeed a conflict, a battle between the *civitas Dei,* the city of God, and *civitas mundi,* the city of the world" (CLPL, 77).

And Christian philosophers must enter that battle, quite explicitly and self-consciously, "*primarily* or *first of all* as members of the Christian community, and only secondarily as members of, say, the philosophical community at large, or the contemporary academic community. Our first responsibility is to the Lord and to the Christian community, not first of all to the philosophical community at large" (CLPL, 78).

We will return to this challenging question, and Plantinga's attempt to answer it, in our look at his methodology in chapter 7.

For Whom Has This Book Been Written?

Perhaps learning about Plantinga's Christian upbringing and education, his teaching career, and his significance and influence in the philosophical world, has whetted your appetite for discovering his distinctive philosophical ideas and arguments. If so, read on; that is the rest of the book. But given the readership at which the Great Thinkers series is aimed, here are three further reasons to be interested in this book.

First, you may have heard of Plantinga and his importance, particularly with respect to the problem of evil and the rationality of belief in God, but you can't understand what he is saying or why it is important. This book is geared to help you out, providing accessible summaries of Plantinga's key moves (the "what") and relating his arguments to a larger cultural context (the "why").

Second, you may have heard that Plantinga is a Calvinist philosopher of some sort, but you don't know what is Calvinistic about him, if anything. Again, this book is intended to help, by highlighting several key doctrines in Reformed systematic theology and several themes in the Reformed tradition of defending the faith, and then explaining to what extent Plantinga adheres to or abandons them.

Third, you may know that Christian pastors, theologians, and other thinkers you trust dispute among themselves whether Plantinga's contributions are a help or a hindrance to the church and its task of reaching the world with the gospel. This book may help you out here, but not in a way that is all or nothing. I take a somewhat eclectic approach in separating the wheat from the chaff, taking what I see as good, and explaining why I leave the rest—all the while encouraging readers to think for themselves on these matters. Hopefully you can gain confidence that it doesn't take a specialist to see the big picture here.

Speaking personally for a moment, I first encountered Plantinga's work as a philosophy undergraduate at UCLA and continued to reflect on it during my years at Westminster Seminary in California and beyond. I've taught a wide range of his monographs and articles for the last twenty years in the seminary classroom among a dozen different classes on a two-year cycle. (Don't worry; I've taught work from other philosophers too!) There are other books devoted to Plantinga's work, but these tend to be devoid of *theological* evaluation (at least from a conservative, evangelical, or Reformed perspective). Likewise, there are Reformed works that cover apologetics, but they do not typically focus on Plantinga's contributions to apologetics and philosophy, despite his immense influence on a global scale. This book focuses on Plantinga and tries to combine philosophical accuracy with theological evaluation, while remaining accessible. As you continue, I hope to deliver on all these fronts!

Over the next five chapters, we will survey Plantinga's ideas on faith and reason, the problem of evil, arguments for God, the divine attributes, and the relationship between religion and science. We'll close by reflecting on his philosophical method and evaluating his relation to the Reformed heritage.

2

PLANTINGA ON FAITH AND REASON

Plantinga's Faculty-Based Approach to Faith and Reason

Faith and Reason as Two Ways of Knowing

The topic of faith and reason is crucial in both Christian apologetics (the defense of the faith) and philosophy of religion (evaluating and articulating arguments for or against the coherence or truth of central religious claims). Typically, pursuing this topic involves examining how faith (understood in a particular way) relates to reason (understood in a particular way). Different relations might hold here, depending on what we take faith or reason to be. Lurking in the background of the historical discussion is a sense, primarily among critics of Christianity, that reason is perfectly fine as it is, but faith simply doesn't measure up to the standards of reason (for some reason!), and because of this conflict, faith is a substandard way of living one's intellectual life. Advocates of faith primarily respond by critiquing the arguments for a conflict between faith and reason. Perhaps the critic has tendentiously defined faith in an idiosyncratic manner that no advocate of faith accepts. For example, faith might be defined, as Mark Twain did, as "believing what you know ain't true." Or the critic might define faith and reason tolerably well, but then sneak in an additional, quite dubious assumption that is desperately in need of support. For instance: it can never be rational to believe in things you can't see. Or a hundred other things can go wrong here. The debate between faith and reason is as ancient, pervasive, and complicated as any other fundamental human inquiry about truth and knowledge.

One way to approach this debate—which is what Plantinga himself does again and again—is to construe faith and reason as *two different ways of knowing*. For instance, perhaps reason is a way of knowing that utilizes our cognitive capacities for perception, memory, insight, introspection, testimony, and inference (both deductive and inductive). Since the following beliefs would be acquired by using such capacities, these beliefs are acquired by reason:

1. "The tree is in the yard beyond my window" (perception).
2. "I had Cheerios for breakfast this morning" (memory).
3. "$2 + 2 = 4$" (insight).
4. "I'm thinking about philosophy right now" (introspection).
5. "Abraham Lincoln was assassinated" (testimony).
6. "Since $2 + 2 = 4$, therefore $2 + 2 \neq 5$" (deductive inference).
7. "Since the sun has always risen in the past, it will probably rise tomorrow" (inductive inference).

By way of contrast, faith is a way of knowing that utilizes two cognitive capacities over and above those just named: a sense of the divine (what Calvin calls the *sensus divinitatis* in his *Institutes,* 1.3.1, first sentence), and a capacity to repose trust in divine testimony. Since the following beliefs would be acquired by using such capacities, these beliefs are acquired by faith:

8. "God is an awesome Creator" (*sensus divinitatis,* said while contemplating a mountain).
9. "God is displeased with what I did" (divine testimony, said while reading the Sermon on the Mount).

Evaluating the Alternatives to the Faculty-Based Approach

These are not, of course, the only ways to characterize faith and reason. Rather than adopting the "faculty-based" approach I've just sketched, someone could urge a "content-based" approach. On this view, the difference between faith and reason is just a matter of the *content* of what is believed: reason-beliefs are about "the empirical world," whereas faith-beliefs are about "an invisible realm." But this approach is an obvious nonstarter. Intuitively, some reason-beliefs are about an invisible realm—for instance, the atheist's belief that God, if he existed, would be unjustified in permitting so much evil as there is in the world. Isn't that a belief about an invisible being? And some faith-beliefs are surely about the empirical world—for instance, the Christian's belief that the world was created by God. Isn't that a belief about the empirical world? So the content-based approach to the distinction between faith and reason seems like a dead end.

But perhaps someone could urge an "inference-based" approach to faith and reason. On this view, a belief is rational if it is inferred from something else—that is, if it is based on good reasons. (This essentially reduces reason to capacities 6 and 7 above.) Then the idea is that faith-beliefs must be those beliefs that are not based on reasons; they are without reasonable support—not rational—because they are held for no reason at all. If they were based on reasons, then they wouldn't be faith-beliefs. But this inference-based approach is just as disastrous as the content-based approach, especially for the advocate of reason. It would follow that the first five kinds of belief listed above—perception, memory, insight, introspection, and testimony—aren't rational or reasonable beliefs, since no one holds them on the basis of other beliefs. Rather, you open your eyes and find yourself believing that the tree is in the yard. Or you think about it, and you find yourself believing that you had Cheerios for breakfast, or that 2 + 2 = 4, and so on. It would also follow from the inference-based approach that any faith-belief would automatically be a reason-belief, if you based it on reasons—such as, if it were inferred from things said in the Bible. But if that's the case, what is the distinction between faith and reason worth?

The Virtues of the Faculty-Based Approach

So let's put aside the content- and inference-based approaches as misguided, and come back to the faculty-based approach to faith and reason, which is the one that Plantinga champions. Capacities 1–7 above produce reason-beliefs and capacities 8–9 produce faith-beliefs. Construing faith and reason in these two ways has several decided advantages.

First, it clearly distinguishes reason from faith, rather than confusing them. Suppose we instead identified faith with a particular content or topic of belief, such as believing in God. Clearly, one can arrive at that belief by way of inference or by way of simple trust. But is it really the case that someone who believes in God on the basis of argument (say, an argument from design) is believing by faith, simply because the belief has a content that is about God? Distinguishing between faith and reason by content just doesn't get us a good distinction; it gets us confusion.

Second, the faculty-based approach, while preserving a distinction between faith and reason, acknowledges strong parallels between knowledge gained by reason and knowledge reached by faith—parallels that are significant for figuring out whether faith conflicts with reason. Notice that empirical perception (way 1) is like the *sensus divinitatis* (way 8). They both involve a belief being formed in certain circumstances (you find yourself having the belief when you are in those circumstances), but the belief isn't inferred from another belief. You reason *from* perceptual beliefs; you don't reason *to* them. In the same way, the sense of the divine is like perception. Similarly, trusting in ordinary human testimony (way 5) is like trusting in divine testimony (way 9). You simply find yourself in the presence of a testifier whom you have no reason to doubt, and you find yourself believing what is said (or written). If ways 1 and 5 are legitimately rational—and what advocate of reason would deny that perception and testimony are sources of rational belief?—then why would ways 8 and 9 be defective? Wouldn't the critic who says that faith is intellectually substandard be guilty of a double standard?

Third, the faculty-based approach provides a nifty explanation of the popular tendency within secular culture to caricature faith as irrational, while exposing that tendency as itself misguided. Faith is often dismissed as believing *without* support, whereas being reasonable is just to believe *with* support. This view is attractive to many people, because they know people of faith who strike them as stubbornly having beliefs that are baseless, and because they know that deductive and inductive inference are examples of rationality *par excellence*. So faith-beliefs are allegedly irrational because they are based on nothing. Nevertheless, this argument for the irrationality of faith has nothing going for it. Beliefs 1–5 above are eminently reasonable, despite not being based on other beliefs. If support is required to have a rational belief, then nothing we believe by way of perception, memory, insight, introspection, or testimony is rational. One would have to reject reason itself to maintain that faith-beliefs are intrinsically irrational—a Pyrrhic victory at best for any critic of faith.

Fourth, the faculty-based approach reveals that many attempts to show a conflict between faith and reason appeal to considerations that are simply irrelevant to generating any such conflict.

For instance, someone might say that faith-beliefs are irrational because their source is something other than the seven sources of reason-beliefs listed above. But this is irrelevant, since a belief having a source other than reason is not the same thing as that belief conflicting with reason. To think otherwise is like saying that, because our memory beliefs proceed from a source other than perception or testimony, our memory beliefs conflict with perception or testimony. No one thinks this. Not all reason-beliefs come from the same source, and they are no worse off for that. The same is true for faith-beliefs. Furthermore, perhaps I can know something by faith that I can't know by reason. That's as unremarkable as the fact that I can know some things by testimony that I can't know by perception (e.g., that you have a headache).

Fifth, the faculty-based approach helps us see more clearly that there is no *noncircular* way of proving the reliability of reason—beliefs. Simply go through faculties 1–7 above and ask yourself how you would demonstrate to yourself or someone else that each particular faculty is reliable? Whatever way you come up with will inevitably involve you relying upon the faculty you are seeking to vindicate—that is, you will go in a circle. Typically, the charge of circularity is made against advocates of faith-beliefs who trust faculties 8–9, but here the shoe is on the other foot.

Sixth, the faculty-based approach allows for something that is quite intuitive from a Christian point of view: some things might be knowable by way of *both* faith and reason. The early apostles could have known of the resurrection of Christ by reason (broadly construed, through perception, way 1 above), and the hearers of Peter's Pentecost sermon could have known of it also by reason (through hearing human testimony, way 5), whereas we who read Scripture today can know of it by faith (through way 9). What exactly is irrational or contradictory about that? We already believe something like this with respect to reason itself: what I had for breakfast might be knowable by perception (if someone observes me at the time), by memory (as I later reflect on it), and by testimony (as someone else hears me recall it).

How Did Plantinga Arrive at This Point of View?

In characterizing faith and reason as two ways of knowing, I have deliberately started at the end of the Plantingian story, as it were, offering you an extended glimpse into the benefits of Plantinga's mature thought on this subject. The preceding exposition of the faculty-based approach was drawn from Plantinga's relatively recent arguments in *WTCRL*, 178–83, and *WCB*, 256–66. It is now time to tell the earlier parts of this story.

Back in the late 1970s, Plantinga began to reflect on an anti-Christian argument that a very paradigmatic faith-belief—namely, belief in God—was positively irrational to hold. This anti-Christian argument is the evidentialist objection to belief in God, and Plantinga's reply to it spelled the start of the "Reformed epistemology" movement.[1] Most significantly, by drawing upon a theme he found in Calvin and other Reformed theologians, Plantinga was able to expose this objection as argumentatively worthless, or at least incomplete. After that, over the next twenty years or so, deeper reflection, not only on Calvin's concept of the *sensus divinitatis*, but also on his concept of *faith as knowledge*, led Plantinga to reconceptualize the rest of epistemology. Eventually, by the late 1990s, Plantinga provided a "proper function" understanding of *all* the deliverances of reason and of *all* the deliverances of faith, giving a unified theory of how *both* kinds of belief can count as warranted true belief, and therefore knowledge. This unified account leads to a strong conclusion: there *cannot* be a fundamental conflict between faith and reason, since reason is just as faith-like as faith, and faith is just as reasonable as reason.

1. See "Is Belief in God Rational?" (IBIGR) from 1979 and "Reason and Belief in God" (RBG) from 1983. Several of Plantinga's key ideas were already expressed in "The Sceptics' Strategy" (SS) from 1965.

These two brothers, separated at birth in our fallen world, are now revealed to be members of the same family: sources of knowledge delivered by God-given faculties, at least when they are functioning properly. The irritating grain of sand in 1979 (the evidentialist objection) eventually produced the pearl of 2000 (the account of reason and faith functioning properly).

That sounds like a tale worth telling! So, let's tell it properly and start at the beginning. My hope is that the jigsaw puzzle pieces will eventually fit together to provide a seamless portrait of faith *and* reason, as opposed to the jagged pile of faith *versus* reason.

The Rise of Reformed Epistemology

In 1983, after arriving at the University of Notre Dame, Plantinga coedited with Nicholas Wolterstorff (his undergraduate classmate at Calvin College in the 1950s) the volume *Faith and Rationality: Reason and Belief in God.* This collection of essays became the *locus classicus* for the "Reformed epistemology" movement, which contended that belief in God could be "properly basic," that is, rational for believers quite apart from any argument in its support. While Christian philosophers such as William Alston ("Christian Experience and Christian Belief") and Nicholas Wolterstorff ("Can Belief in God Be Rational If It Has No Foundations?") were among the contributors, it was Plantinga's lengthy essay in that volume, "Reason and Belief in God" (RBG), which had the most enduring influence on how the movement was perceived.

Step 1: The Evidentialist Objection to Belief in God Is Rooted in Classical Foundationalism

In the space of nearly eighty pages, Plantinga responds to the "evidentialist objection" to the rationality of theistic belief. This objection says that the theist, to be rational, must have sufficient evidence for the existence of God, and that evidence must take the form of a good argument for God's existence. Plantinga responds with a simple question: why should anyone believe this? To answer this question, Plantinga offers an epistemological excavation of Western philosophy, seeking to discern the intellectual standards at work in the ancient, medieval, and modern eras when the rationality of theistic belief was the topic of discussion. He discovers that in each era the evidentialist objection was grounded in a prior theory of rationality that he calls "classical foundationalism." That's not to say that the phrase "classical foundationalism" was used throughout history, but that a particular set of ideas (which Plantinga *calls* "classical foundationalism") was typically assumed when thinkers raised the evidentialist objection against belief in God.

As a theory of rationality, classical foundationalism (CF) doesn't say that *every* rational belief must be supported by, or based on, prior argument. That would be extreme and implausible; there must be some starting point for thought! CF says that *some* beliefs can be rational without argument—that is, "proper" to hold as "basic" beliefs. But these basic beliefs are going to be very special categories of belief, and belief in God isn't one of them. There are three categories of basic belief, according to CF. First, it's OK to accept *self-evident beliefs* without argument; these beliefs, as soon as you understand the claim that is being presented by them, strike you as obviously true. For example, "If something is red, then it has a color." Second, it's OK to accept *sensory beliefs* without argument; these beliefs are simple deliverances of your five senses. For example, "I see the clock." Third, it's OK to accept *incorrigible beliefs* without argument; these beliefs are about your inward mental states. For example, "It seems to me that I see a tree." According to CF, these are the only three categories of belief that may be properly accepted in a basic way, that is, without argument.

What this means is that, according to CF, belief in God can't be basic. After all, it's not self-evident; you can understand it without accepting it. It's not a sensory belief; you can't perceive God with any of the five senses. And it's not an incorrigible belief; it's not about your inward mental experience. Since belief in God can't be a basic belief, it must be a *based* belief—that is, a belief based on argument—in order to be rational. And this is the standard of rationality to which the evidentialist objection appeals. Unless you can set forth an argument, on the basis of which you believe in God, your belief in God is positively irrational. Thus, in classical foundationalism, theistic belief has to be supported by argument if it is to be accepted as rational.

Step 2: Classical Foundationalism Is Obviously False and Incoherent

In response, Plantinga argues that CF (the theory of rationality assumed in the evidentialist objection) is doubly defective: "It turns out to be both false and self-referentially incoherent" (RBG, 90). First, CF is too narrow and therefore obviously false. There are plenty of paradigmatically rational beliefs that anyone would accept as properly basic, even though they don't conform to CF's three categories for basic belief. For example, memory beliefs—such as "I had Cheerios for breakfast this morning"—aren't self-evident, or evident to the senses, or incorrigible. So, according to CF, they're not properly basic. But they're not based beliefs either. We don't base them on argument, saying to ourselves, "I'm having a memory-like experience right now of having Cheerios; usually when I have that experience, it's because I did eat Cheerios; so, on the basis of this argument, I'm going to go ahead and believe that I had Cheerios." That's exactly what we don't do. Rather, we just think about it, have a memory experience of some sort, and find ourselves believing we had Cheerios. It's a basic belief. (Plantinga argues the same for our beliefs grounded in testimony, our belief in an external world, our belief in other persons, and so on.) But CF would exclude memory beliefs, testimony beliefs, and all those other kinds of obviously basic and rational beliefs as irrational. Since most of what we know, we know by way of memory and testimony, CF would imply that everyone is irrational in most of what they believe. That's a pretty poor theory of rational belief. It can't be right.

Second, and even worse, CF is self-referentially incoherent. That is, if it were the correct theory of rationality, we would thereby have good reason to reject it. Take CF to stand for the following belief: "To be rational, a belief must be self-evident, or evident to the senses, or incorrigible, or based on beliefs like that." But what about *that* belief (the one in between the quotation marks)? Is it rational? CF would have to say "no." After all, CF isn't a properly *based* belief, one for which we can give a good argument. And CF isn't a properly *basic* belief, since CF itself doesn't fall into any of its three categories of proper (or allowable) basic belief: it's not self-evident, evident to our empirical senses, or incorrigible. So, by its own standards of rationality, CF should be rejected as irrational. That's a pretty unstable theory of rationality! Plantinga concludes that the evidentialist objection just isn't cogent. Theists have nothing to fear from seriously defective theories of rationality like classical foundationalism. Nor should they fear any objections that rely upon it.

Step 3: The Possibility of Properly Basic Belief in God through the *Sensus Divinitatis*

Plantinga points out that, so far as the objector has argued, at the very least it could be the case that belief in God is properly basic and therefore just as rational as self-evident belief, sensory belief, incorrigible belief, memory belief, testimony belief, and so on. Why not? Indeed, it may very well be the case, as Calvin seems to think in Book I of the *Institutes,* that God has given us a *sensus divinitatis* (a "sense of the divine") analogous to sense perception. This would supply us with properly basic belief in God that is justified quite apart from argument. Does the critic have a good argument that God hasn't done this? You won't find such an argument in the evidentialist objection! Perhaps God has designed us in such a way that I am rational in spontaneously believing that "a beautiful God made this" when contemplating the beauty of a flower, or believing that "a majestic God made this" when contemplating the grandeur of a mountain, or believing that "God is displeased with what I have done" when contemplating some selfish act of mine from earlier in the day. I don't argue my way to these theistic beliefs. I *find myself* with them, because of how God has made me. They're perfectly normal and straightforward; the defective, unworthy, and irrational thing to do would be to suppress these beliefs.

It is important to stress that Plantinga isn't arguing by way of this so-called Reformed epistemology that God exists. He isn't even arguing that belief in God is properly basic. Rather, he's showing that one argument that belief in God isn't rational, isn't a good argument. That's it. That might seem insignificant, but the implications are in fact enormous, for at least three reasons.

First, Plantinga is showing that allegedly neutral criteria of rationality, according to which traditional religious beliefs are assessed as intellectually suspect, typically hide an anti-religious animus or at least bias. In particular, theories of rationality that declare theistic belief to be irrational unless supported by deductive or inductive argument are themselves either incoherent or obviously false. Plantinga is engaging in an important activity of wide relevance: Christian apologists and philosophers need to train themselves to focus on and challenge key assumptions made by critics, even if such assumptions strike many as commonsense. (Plantinga has discerned that classical foundationalism has been characteristic of much thought in the ancient, medieval, and modern eras, despite being defective.)

Second, Reformed epistemology is a way of beginning a conversation that is crucial for both believers and unbelievers:

epistemology might depend on theology. If so, this might place important limits on what we can show by way of philosophy alone. Do we have the *sensus divinitatis*? Did God create us to spontaneously form belief in him in a wide variety of circumstances, as a normal part of human nature? Abstract theories of rationality may not be of help here. What matters is what God did, and that might be answerable only by theology.

Third, Reformed epistemology is an interesting example of starting with Christian belief and then developing a larger philosophical theory that applies the Christian belief and considers its implications. In this case, the Christian belief is something Calvin says in the *Institutes* about how we get knowledge of God. If what Calvin says is right, if God has given us a sense that functions to give us knowledge of God, then maybe that is a clue to the rest of the knowing process as creatures made in the image of God. And now we have arrived at the next part of the Plantingian story.[2]

The Journey to *Warranted Christian Belief*

Warrant: The Current Debate and *Warrant and Proper Function* (1993)

The Reformed epistemology of 1983 had a rather narrow focus when it came to the nature and scope of knowledge. By merely defending the *rationality* of belief in God, Plantinga was assuming that rationality was important and perhaps even central to the nature of knowledge. But perhaps it's not. And perhaps

2. Just how Reformed is Reformed epistemology? We'll consider that question in chapter 8 when we look at the Reformed heritage. Suffice it to say that both terms might be misnomers. As Plantinga himself would later discover, the idea that belief in God can be basic is not the peculiar property of the Reformed tradition. Similar things are said in Aquinas. As for epistemology, Reformed epistemology isn't one. It's not a theory of knowledge in any traditional sense; it's just an argument that one objection to the rationality of belief in God doesn't work.

justification isn't crucial either, if by that we mean some feature of our beliefs that we can just see, and that gives us the right to hold our beliefs. Rather, what might be really important for knowledge is proper function. And by merely defending the rationality of *belief in God,* the Reformed epistemology project had a very narrow scope. What about the rest of knowledge and belief? How should a Christian think about that?

Starting in 1993, Plantinga sought to remedy this twofold limitation in the Reformed epistemology project by publishing a series of volumes that much more robustly developed his ideas about the nature of knowledge and then applied that theory of knowledge to a much wider scope of knowledge claims (beyond belief in God). The first volume of Plantinga's trilogy on warrant, *Warrant: The Current Debate* (*WCD*), sought to show that the nature of knowledge doesn't really depend on rationality or justification, as these have been traditionally conceived. This first volume was a kind of prolegomenon that sought to knock down popular and influential alternatives to the theory of warrant that Plantinga would eventually propose. Here, "warrant" is taken to be what true beliefs need to have if they are to be knowledge. Plantinga argues in *WCD* that warrant isn't justification or rationality. So what is it then?

The second volume of Plantinga's trilogy, *Warrant and Proper Function* (*WPF*) (1993), seeks to answer that question, arguing that warrant is *proper function.* In short, "a belief has warrant if it is produced by cognitive faculties functioning properly (subject to no malfunctioning) in a cognitive environment congenial for those faculties, according to a design plan successfully aimed at truth" (*WPF*, viii–ix). Given this theory of what is most important for knowledge, Plantinga goes on to reconceive the nature of knowledge along these lines, not just with respect to belief in God, but with respect to all kinds of knowledge: perception, memory, insight, introspection, testimony, deductive inference, and inductive inference. Notice that these are reasoning capacities 1–7, as distinguished earlier in this chapter.[3]

Warranted Christian Belief **(2000)**

The third volume of Plantinga's trilogy, *Warranted Christian Belief* (*WCB*), applies his proper function theory of warrant to beliefs produced by faith, rather than by reason, showing that they too can count as knowledge. He first considers belief in God by way of the *sensus divinitatis* (way 8), articulating an Aquinas/Calvin (A/C) model of theistic belief. According to the A/C model, God has given us a faculty for perceiving God that is analogous to sense perception (way 1). If the *sensus divinitatis* gives us true beliefs, and it is functioning properly in an appropriate environment according to a design plan successfully aimed at truth, then it gives us knowledge of God. Like perception, this would be a basic belief (not based on argument), but it would still be knowledge.

Of course, according to the Christian faith, we live in a fallen world, and that affects our mind, along with the rest of our being and our environment. This has two unfortunate consequences. First, many of us *don't* form basic belief in God by way of the *sensus divinitatis*; or, if we do, we don't admit it to ourselves or others. Rather, we "suppress the truth in unrighteousness" (Romans 1:18 NASB). Because of the fall, we are subject to cognitive malfunction, and so the *sensus divinitatis* doesn't get us knowledge of God (or not in the way or to the extent it ought). Second, the only remedy for our fallen condition is to believe (as Plantinga often puts it) "the great things of the gospel"—Trinity, incarnation, atonement, justification by faith in Christ—but we suppress that truth as well.

3. Interestingly, the order of treatment in *WPF* is different: introspection, memory, testimony, perception, insight, inductive inference, and deductive inference. Plantinga offers a very accessible, four-page summary of his theory of "warrant as proper function" in *KCB*, 25–28, a 2015 book that is itself a concise summary of his entire epistemology.

The fall is so debilitating that we aren't inclined to read the Bible or listen to Christian preachers, or when we do, we rebel against or otherwise ignore this divine testimony and remain in unbelief.

To remedy these two effects of the fall (which are both cognitive and affective, having to do with the mind and the will), we need a powerful work of the Holy Spirit, inclining our minds and hearts to receive, understand, and repose our confidence in divine testimony about the great things of the gospel. In short, we need to be converted; we need Christian faith. And since Christian faith is a form of knowledge (way 9), it can be analyzed as such by Plantinga's proper function account. Here he articulates an "extended A/C model" of gospel belief (and not merely theistic belief), according to which the "internal instigation of the Holy Spirit" is a kind of properly functioning process that produces Christian faith. And because this work of the Holy Spirit satisfies the conditions of warrant, as Plantinga has defined it, Christian faith is a form of knowledge. Analogous to way 5, it arises in the presence of testimony. Arguments for God or for the truth of the Bible are not needed for Christian faith. Someone can acquire saving faith in the gospel merely by reading his Bible or listening to a sermon, even if he has never heard of Justin Martyr, Thomas Aquinas, C. S. Lewis, or any other defender of the faith. Just as Plantinga argued in 1983 that belief in God could be properly basic, so in 2000 he argued the same for the full panoply of distinctive Christian belief. Further, we now see that both kinds of belief can not only be properly basic, but also count as *knowledge*.

Implications for Christian Apologetics

There is a decidedly Christian apologetical slant to how Plantinga presents the epistemological material in this third volume. Not content with merely articulating a Christian theory of knowledge, he applies it to show that many criticisms of Christian belief beg the question against the Christian believer. The main thesis of *Warranted Christian Belief* is that there is a link between two questions: the *de facto* question of whether Christian belief is *true*, and the *de jure* question of whether it is *warranted*. Plantinga argues that his proper function account of Christian belief has now shown that if Christian belief is true, then it is warranted. (The Bible itself gives the rough outlines of the view that the *sensus divinitatis* and the internal instigation of the Holy Spirit are the sources of belief in God and in the gospel, respectively. Plantinga is just showing that these phenomena satisfy the standards for knowledge.)

But if Christian belief is warranted, if true, then if someone says it isn't warranted, they are virtually assuming that it isn't true—because if it were true, it would be warranted, as Plantinga has argued. So any argument that Christian belief isn't warranted presupposes that Christian belief isn't true. This line of thought is of great significance for Christian apologetics: if Plantinga is right, then many critics' arguments aren't ways of *showing* that Christianity is false; they're ways of *presupposing* that Christianity is false. They just assume that Christian belief doesn't tell us the right story of how we get faith. But what if it does?

To argue against Christianity, then, the critic will just have to straightforwardly argue that it is false. Many such "defeaters" of the truth of Christianity have been offered over the past two thousand years, such as Freudian projective theories of religious belief, higher biblical criticism, postmodernist rejection of objective truth, pluralism about religious belief, and the problem of evil. In the last part of *Warranted Christian Belief*, Plantinga examines each of these defeaters, arguing that not one of them is in fact successful as an argument against Christian belief. Since these direct ways of showing that Christianity is false are not cogent, then—all things considered—we have no good reason for thinking that faith isn't a form of knowledge.[4]

4. This material in Part IV of *WCB* is of independent interest as an extended exercise in Christian apologetics, and we will return to Plantinga's response to the problem of evil in the next chapter.

Implications for How Theology Relates to Philosophy

The early project in Reformed epistemology combines with the later project in proper function epistemology in a way that is quite significant for the topic with which this chapter began: faith and reason and how the two relate. We can summarize these implications with two slogans: "Faith is a kind of knowledge," and "Epistemology depends on theology."

First, throughout his career, Plantinga has explicitly derived his notion of faith as a kind of knowledge from Calvin himself. One who believes in God by way of the *sensus divinitatis,* "says Calvin, *knows* that God exists" (RBG, 67). In addition, the idea that faith in the truth of the gospel is also a kind of knowledge is also derived from Calvin:

> Faith, says Calvin, is "a firm and certain knowledge of God's benevolence towards us, founded upon the truth of the freely given promise in Christ, both revealed to our minds and sealed upon our hearts through the Holy Spirit" (*Institutes* III, ii, 7, p. 551). Faith therefore involves an explicitly cognitive element; it is, says Calvin, *knowledge*—knowledge of the availability of redemption and salvation through the person and work of Jesus Christ—and it is revealed to our minds. To have faith, therefore, is to know and hence *believe* something or other. (*WCB*, 244)

Or again:

> It is not that the deliverances of faith are to be contrasted with *knowledge*; according to John Calvin, faith "is a firm and certain *knowledge* of God's benevolence towards us." So a proposition I believe by faith can (at least according to followers of Calvin) nonetheless be something I know." (*WTCRL*, 179, quoting *Institutes* III.ii.7)

Second, the conclusion that the *de jure* question of warrant depends on the *de facto* question of truth is a genuine and substantive development in Plantinga's epistemological position, and it teaches us something highly important about how theology relates to philosophy:

> And here we see the ontological or metaphysical or ultimately religious roots of the question as to the rationality or warrant or lack thereof for belief in God. What you properly take to be rational, at least in the sense of warranted, depends on what sort of metaphysical and religious stance you adopt. It depends on what kind of beings you think human beings are, what sorts of beliefs you think their noetic faculties will produce when they are functioning properly, and which of their faculties or cognitive mechanisms are aimed at the truth. Your view as to what sort of creature a human being is will determine or at any rate heavily influence your views as to whether theistic belief is warranted or not warranted, rational or irrational for human beings. And so the dispute as to whether theistic belief is rational (warranted) can't be settled just by attending to epistemological considerations; *it is at bottom not merely an epistemological dispute, but an ontological or theological dispute*." (*WCB*, 190, emphasis added)

Conclusion

We've now arrived at the end of our story. We began that story at the end, by explaining a faculty-based approach to faith and reason and its advantages. We then saw the two-step process by which Plantinga arrives at that approach. He starts by considering the implications of just one cognitive faculty that it is possible for humans to have: the *sensus divinitatis*. Plantinga's Dutch Reformed upbringing brought him into contact with the writing of Calvin and other Reformed theologians on the knowledge of God. The mere possibility of this cognitive faculty throws a wrench into the machinery of the whole evidentialist objection. That objection simply assumes (but does not show) that belief in God couldn't be properly basic. In fact, it assumes a picture of rational belief that is so narrow that it implausibly excludes as irrational lots of other rational beliefs that the evidentialist objector accepts. Worse still, the picture of rational belief is self-referentially incoherent.

But now consider this. If belief in God produced by the *sensus divinitatis* can be entirely rational as a properly basic belief ("God simply made me in such a way that I form theistic beliefs in the right circumstances"), then that's only because the *sensus divinitatis* is just as good a sense—intellectually speaking—as our ordinary sense perception. Could it be that that's how the human intellect generally works? Perhaps *we acquire knowledge because that's how God made us,* and all that's left is to consider in more detail *how God made us.* We're not very far from Plantinga's proper function epistemology, in which knowledge crucially depends on how God made us. Once we see that the variety of kinds of knowledge we have is rightly correlated with the enormous variety of cognitive faculties with which we have been equipped, we are led to the faculty-based approach to knowledge with which we started this chapter. It turns out that the best way to construe faith and reason is as two different ways of knowing. It also turns out that this approach is very robust from the standpoint of Christian apologetics. Many attempts to show that faith is irrational are dead on arrival, barely disguised bluster designed more to intimidate than to illuminate.

It also follows that not a single important thing we believe as Christians has to be based on argument in order to be intellectually proper or consistent with reason: not our belief in God, or belief in the Bible, or belief in the great things of the gospel. These can all be produced by the *sensus divinitatis* when we are aware of creation or produced by the internal instigation of the Holy Spirit when considering verbal divine revelation. Could the psychological strength and intellectual rationality of such faith be increased by way of argument? Of course! Nothing in Plantinga's epistemology stands against this. Could that strengthening come from Van Til's transcendental argument, or Aquinas's deductive natural theology, or Swinburne's probabilistic natural theology, or C. S. Lewis's moral argument for God, or W. L. Craig's kalam argument? Again, yes, insofar as any of those arguments are good ones (and, for the record, I think they all are). But, strictly speaking, none of that is *needed* for a faith that pleases God, unites one to Christ for salvation, and sanctifies one in the Christian life. Knowing that might bring needed relief and blessing to many contemporary Christians, and also keep certain would-be critics at bay. Plantinga's framework might also encourage Christian philosophers and apologists to get on with the work of positively relating faith to reason, now that we can see the territory a bit more clearly because of him.

3

PLANTINGA ON THE PROBLEM OF EVIL

The problem of evil is one of the most challenging objections to the Christian faith, a faith which insists that a perfectly good God exists despite the pain and suffering in the world. It is also one of the most discussed objections, and Christian attempts to answer it are legion. Plantinga has put his two mites into this treasury of scholarship, and his contributions have reshaped how the problem gets talked about by philosophers. (Indeed, whether his proposed solutions are good ones takes up a fair bit of the discussion!)

The problem of evil is fundamentally *an argument against God*—specifically, a piece of reasoning which says that the evil in the world gives us good reason to think that God doesn't exist. Here "evil" typically refers to any significant case of pain and suffering.[1] In what follows, we will consider Plantinga's multiple replies to the two most widely discussed forms of the problem of evil: the "logical"

1. Thus Christian apologist C. S. Lewis's book on the problem of evil is called *The Problem of Pain* (New York: Macmillan, 1962).

problem and the "evidential" problem. Plantinga's approach provides an excellent example of how Christian apologetics can draw upon the best theories philosophy has to offer about the nature of possibility, knowledge, probability, and value. The full range of tools and insights offered by all the subdisciplines of philosophy can effectively serve the church in her divinely mandated task of defending the faith. But Plantinga's approach also illustrates that you can't get something for nothing, and some of the assumptions that Plantinga has deployed to defeat the argument have struck others as theologically problematic.

The Logical Problem of Evil

Mackie's Argument

The logical problem of evil has roots going back to the ancient Greek philosopher Epicurus and the Enlightenment skeptic David Hume. Standing in this tradition, the celebrated Oxford atheist J. L. Mackie contended in 1955 that "the problem of evil . . . is a logical problem": religious beliefs "are positively irrational" because "the several parts of the essential theological doctrine are *inconsistent* with one another."[2] In particular, "God is omnipotent," "God is wholly good," and "evil exists" are an inconsistent triad; "if any two of them were true the third would be false."[3]

Mackie's version of the problem says that evil makes the existence of God impossible. Any evil (of any amount) logically contradicts the existence of God. A world with both God and evil is as impossible as a world with an irresistible force and an immovable object. Crucial for Mackie's argument is his definition of two key terms. On his view, "omnipotence" implies that "there are no limits to what an omnipotent thing can do," and "good"

2. J. L. Mackie, "Evil and Omnipotence," *Mind* 64, no. 254 (April 1955): 200.
3. Mackie, "Evil and Omnipotence," 200.

implies that "a good thing always eliminates evil as far as it can."[4] So, if God were both omnipotent and good, there wouldn't be any evil. But obviously there is evil. Thus, no omnipotent, good being exists, which means that God doesn't exist.

This argument is no more complicated than this relatively small number of claims. But the power of the logical problem of evil is supposed to lie in its simplicity. As Hume would say, "Nothing can shake the solidity of this reasoning, so short, so clear, so decisive."[5]

Undercutting Defeater: Mackie Hasn't Made His Case (1974)

Plantinga tackled this formidable logical problem in two ways. In fact, he did so in two books published in 1974: *The Nature of Necessity* (*NN*) and *God, Freedom, and Evil* (*GFE*). The second book was a kind of simplification of the first one, which contained the material "in more rigorous and complete form" (*GFE*, 4). Plantinga's first reply to Mackie is an "undercutting defeater." That is, it doesn't show that Mackie's conclusion—that the existence of evil contradicts the existence of God—is false. Rather, it merely shows that Mackie's conclusion is *inadequately supported.*

Plantinga contends that Mackie's argument requires the following assumption: "An omnipotent and omniscient good being eliminates every evil that it can properly eliminate." Here to "properly" eliminate means to do so "without either eliminating an outweighing good or bringing about a greater evil." Obviously, one could *improperly* eliminate an evil, say, by cutting off someone's leg to remove his painful bruise. But that would only bring about a worse evil, and a good being wouldn't do that. God will only *properly* eliminate evils.

4. Mackie, "Evil and Omnipotence," 201.

5. David Hume, *Dialogues concerning Natural Religion* (London, 1779), 10.34.

But if that's how it is, then Mackie must add an additional assumption to his argument: "If God is omniscient and omnipotent, then he can properly eliminate every evil state of affairs." And that assumption is clearly false. It is easy to come up with dozens of examples of evil states of affairs that cannot be properly eliminated, even by an omniscient and omnipotent being. Plantinga names two: "creative moral heroism in the face of suffering and adversity" and "someone's bearing pain magnificently" (*GFE*, 23). These are both overall good states of affairs that are good precisely because they respond to and overcome evil. If God were to eliminate the evil in these states of affairs, he would also eliminate the good, because the good is defined as that which responds to the evil. So, he can't properly eliminate the evil, despite being omniscient and omnipotent.

It is very important to note that this isn't due to a defect in God. Rather, Plantinga is making a logical point: some states of affairs are overall good because they *include* evils that are overcome by good. By definition, then (and not because of any weakness in God), the evils in these states of affairs are not properly eliminable.[6] Because Mackie hasn't argued (and really, can't argue) that all evils in the world are "properly eliminable," he hasn't successfully argued for a logical contradiction between God and evil.

Rebutting Defeater: Overturning Mackie's Conclusion (the Free Will Defense) (1974)

Why didn't Plantinga stop right here, with his undercutting defeater of Mackie? Isn't it a significant result that Mackie's argument isn't a good one? Yes, but Plantinga wants to do more: to argue that no arguments like Mackie's will work. Plantinga wants

6. As Plantinga puts it, "Certain kinds of values, certain familiar kinds of good states of affairs, can't exist apart from evil of some sort" (*GFE*, 23). Some other examples: compassion, forgiveness, and patience, all in response to various evils.

to rule out in advance all Mackie-style arguments, proving once and for all that God and evil are logically consistent. He wants to prove that Mackie's conclusion is *false*. For that, he needs a "rebutting defeater," an argument that overturns a conclusion and doesn't merely show that it is inadequately supported.

Well, how would you show that two claims—"God exists" and "evil exists"—are logically consistent? What you do, says Plantinga, is "provide a model": to prove *p* and *q* consistent, find a *possibly* true claim *r* that is consistent with *p* and together with *p* entails *q*. It is then seen that *p, q,* and *r* can all be true together. (That's because *p* and *r* being true requires that *q* be true as well, since the former entail the latter.) Since *p* and *q* can both be true simultaneously, they are logically consistent.

Here's an analogy. I tell you that *p,* I am a good person, and that *q,* I voluntarily inflict pain on little children while adults pay me and watch. How can these claims be reconciled? Aren't they contradictory? Am I not a moral monster and therefore not a good person? No, because perhaps *r* is also true: I am a dentist. Clearly, *p* and *r* are consistent (there can be good dentists), and taken together they entail *q* (at least if I do my job and typical dental things happen while the parents watch). So *p* and *q* are consistent, and we have just proved it.

Similarly, Plantinga is on a hunt for a possibly true *r* that is consistent with *p,* God exists, and together with *p* entails *q,* evil exists. What could that *r* be? Here is Plantinga's answer (paraphrased for simplicity):

> *r:* For any free creature available to God to create, that creature is such that if it were to be created, it would do at least one morally bad thing.

Plantinga isn't arguing that *r* is true, just that it's *possibly true.* Imagine that there are truths that reveal to God how all possible persons would use their free will, if they were to be created and placed in specific circumstances. These are contingent truths that could be otherwise. They are also truths that aren't up to God. (One might say: how creatures use their free will is up to them.) Now imagine that this set of truths reveals the sad truth of *r* above. That's not a disaster; many creatures, perhaps most creatures, would end up doing many good things, maybe even most of the time. But according to *r*, at least *once* in their lives, if any of them were created, they would each do a bad thing. And that's just how it is if *r* is true. So, let's say that

> *p:* God exists and creates a world with moral good in it.

You can't get a world with moral good unless God creates free creatures. But if *r* is true, then *p* and *r* will entail that

> *q:* There is evil.

And we're done. By utilizing the possibility talked about in *r*—which Plantinga rather whimsically calls "transworld depravity"—we have proved that God and evil are logically consistent. Plantinga's "free will defense" (FWD) doesn't merely undercut Mackie, but refutes him. Mackie made an extremely ambitious claim: God and evil cannot coexist in any possible world. And the ambitiousness of that claim might be its fatal weakness, because in order to refute it, all you need to find is one possible world in which God and evil coexist. And Plantinga claims to have done so.[7]

7. Although the main statement of Plantinga's two replies to the logical problem of evil is in the two books published in 1974, many of the essential ideas for both were already in place in chapters 5 and 6 of his 1967 book *God and Other Minds* (*GOM*), and chapter 6 of the latter drew upon an even earlier 1965 article, "The Free Will Defense" (TFWD).

Evaluation

Plantinga's twofold response to Mackie's logical problem of evil provoked an enormous amount of literature discussing it. Remarkably, even the atheist Mackie acknowledged that since Plantinga's FWD "is formally possible . . . we can concede that the problem of evil does not, after all, show that the central doctrines of theism are logically inconsistent with one another."[8] That's quite an admission. And a near consensus has emerged that Plantinga did decisively refute the logical problem, thereby shifting philosophers' attention to the very different "evidential" argument discussed below. But does the FWD work?

Here are four concerns, all of which stem from Plantinga's apparent assumption that the relevant kind of freedom is *libertarian*, according to which creatures are free to do otherwise in the same exact circumstances. Such freedom is controversial, according to Reformed Christians (and, interestingly enough, Mackie himself). First, is libertarian free will (LFW) actual? Second, is LFW even possible? Third, are truths about how we would use LFW possible? Fourth, isn't *r* just flatly incompatible with God's omnipotence? We will return to these four questions in chapter 8, on Plantinga and the Reformed heritage. Note that even if the FWD is a miserable failure (for either philosophical or theological reasons), we still have Plantinga's first reply to the logical argument: his undercutting defeater. And perhaps that is all that is needed.

The Evidential Problem of Evil

Rowe's Argument

The atheist William Rowe conceded in 1979 that Plantinga had solved Mackie's "logical" problem of evil, and instead put forth an

8. J. L. Mackie, *The Miracle of Theism: Arguments for and against the Existence of God* (Oxford University Press, 1982), 154.

"evidential" problem of evil: cases of apparently pointless animal suffering provide substantial *evidence* (i.e., rational support) for rejecting the existence of God, even if they do not disprove his existence altogether. According to the initial statement of the argument:

> Factual premise: There exist instances of pointless evil.
> Moral premise: God would prevent pointless evil.
> Conclusion: God doesn't exist.

By "pointless evil," Rowe is referring to "instances of intense suffering which an omnipotent, omniscient being could have prevented without thereby losing some greater good or permitting some evil equally bad or worse."[9] Let's simplify this: an evil is "pointless" if God permitted it, but he didn't *need* to permit it in order to enable a greater good to occur, or to block a worse evil from occurring. The idea behind the moral premise is that a morally good God would prevent these kinds of evils. God will only allow evils that are "greater-good-enablers" or "worse-evil-blockers." He will only allow evils that have a point.[10]

But Rowe insists that his "factual premise" is very likely to be true. Surely there is at least some evil in the world that isn't needed as a greater-good-enabler or worse-evil-blocker. Isn't that obvious? For instance, some animals suffer greatly by burning to death in a forest fire. What point could that serve? Or what about rape, child abuse, or torture for the fun of it? It's highly likely that at least some (if not all) of that is pointless. Such evil doesn't make the world better; indeed, the world is worse off because God didn't prevent it. Therefore, it's highly likely that God doesn't exist.

9. William L. Rowe, "The Problem of Evil and Some Varieties of Atheism," *American Philosophical Quarterly* 16, no. 4 (October 1979): 336.

10. Other terms that get used here, besides "pointless evil," are "gratuitous evil" and "meaningless evil." These are all roughly synonymous. These are evils that aren't needed to accomplish greater goods or to block worse evils.

Notice that Rowe's argument is different from Mackie's because it makes a more modest claim: evil makes the existence of God *unlikely*—though not, strictly speaking, impossible. That is, the amount of evil in the world, or the horrific nature of some of it, is good evidence against the existence of God, so much so that it is very improbable that God exists, and therefore quite irrational to believe that he does exist. There might be justification for God's permitting some of the evil in the world, but it's highly unlikely that all of it is justified.

During his career, Plantinga has tackled the evidential problem of evil (whether found in Rowe or others) in at least five ways: by contextualizing it within a broader range of evidence, by adapting his FWD to answer it, by critiquing the probability theory used in it, by endorsing "skeptical theism," and by endorsing supralapsarian theodicy. Each of these approaches is extremely interesting, but space only permits a sketch of each.

First Reply: Contextualizing the Problem within a Broader Range of Evidence (1979)

First, Plantinga asks what would follow for rational belief in God if Christians *concede everything* to the atheist here. Let's say the evidential argument is sound, evidentially speaking. What would follow? That it is irrational to believe in God? Not by a long shot. Even if God's existence is unlikely with respect to some things we know (namely, evil), it wouldn't follow that God's existence is unlikely with respect to everything we know. Maybe the likelihood of God's existence does "take a hit," as it were, from the problem of evil. Evil makes God's existence less likely. Still, maybe the likelihood of God's existence is more than bolstered by the incredibly diverse and substantial array of evidence for his existence that is available to us. Perhaps the pro-God evidence overwhelms and more than compensates for any anti-God evidence to which the atheist points.

Plantinga's own analogy, first expressed in 1979 in "The Probabilistic Argument from Evil" (PAFE), is humorous and insightful. How likely is it that "Feike can swim?" Well, that depends on what evidence we're looking at. If the only thing we know about Feike is that "Feike is a Frisian and 9 out of 10 Frisians can't swim," then—with respect to that piece of information alone—it's pretty improbable that Feike can swim. (That's similar to how it is with the problem of evil.) But what if I have access to a broader range of evidence about Feike? What if I know in addition that "Feike is a Frisian lifeguard and 99 out of 100 Frisian lifeguards can swim"? Now everything changes. It is now very likely that Feike can swim, since I'm consulting this expanded range of evidence. (That's similar to how it is when we look at theistic arguments.) So, it's not as if the problem of evil shows, all by itself, that it is irrational to believe in God. It depends on what other evidence is available. (Plantinga's own commitment to theistic arguments will be examined in the next chapter.)

Second Reply: Adapting the Free Will Defense (1974)

Second, Plantinga shrewdly adapts his FWD—originally invented to refute the logical problem of evil—so that it undermines the evidential problem of evil. What atheists like Rowe are saying is that, if we look at the various evils in the world, we should conclude that "it is unlikely or improbable that the actual world is the best of all possible worlds" (*GFE*, 61). Allegedly, it is very likely that God could have done better. Evil is a kind of evidence that shows us God could have done better. But if they really mean that, they will have to hold that the following claim is very unlikely to be true:

> NBB ("no better balance"): "God is omniscient, omnipotent, and morally perfect; God has created the world; all the evil in the world is broadly moral evil; and there is no possible world

> God could have created that contains a better balance of broadly moral good with respect to broadly moral evil." (*GFE*, 63)

By "broadly moral evil," Plantinga means to include the freely willed evil of nonhuman agents, such as fallen angels, and by "broadly moral good," Plantinga means to include the freely willed good of nonhuman agents, such as unfallen angels. Further, "broadly moral evil" includes "natural evil": it is demons who cause hurricanes, tornadoes, earthquakes, etc. All evil would be (broadly) moral evil, brought about by the abuse of human or angelic free will.

If NBB is true, then there is "no better balance" of good and evil available in any world God could have created, than the balance of good and evil that we find in our actual world. So, God can't be blamed for not doing better. Of course, atheists will regard NBB as an outrageous claim! All natural evils are due to demons? Truths about how creatures (both human and angelic) would use their freedom are such that God couldn't have created a better world, one with more good and less evil? Ridiculous!

But Plantinga holds his ground: what evidence do atheists have against NBB? After all, the problem of evil is their argument, and the burden of proof is with them—he who affirms must prove. How do they know that NBB is unlikely? Unless they know this, they can't know that it's likely God could do better! It's not as if there's some "cosmic book" in which atheists can look up propositions like NBB and see that they're unlikely. As it stands, atheists have no evidence against the truth of NBB. It follows that atheists are too ignorant to advance the evidential problem of evil. They don't have access to any evidence for or against NBB. Their ignorance means that they don't know if the evil in the world makes God's existence unlikely or not.[11]

11. Though few people note this, Plantinga's strategy in his 1974 reply to the evidential argument anticipated by at least ten years the "skeptical theist" strategy made popular by Stephen Wykstra (1984) and others (see below). Essential to both

Third Reply: Critiquing Probability Theory (1979, 1988)

Third, beginning in 1979 ("The Probabilistic Argument from Evil"), Plantinga has examined in great detail the idea that claims about evil can make the claim that God exists unlikely or improbable. What concept of probability are we talking about, and is the problem of evil cogent on any extant theory of probability? To introduce his discussion, Plantinga notes:

> There are nowadays three important interpretations of the probability calculus (with several sub-varieties of each): the *logical* interpretation, according to which the probability relation is a quasi-logical relation of which entailment is a special case, the *frequency* interpretation which holds that probability statements essentially record the relative frequency of events of one sort among events of another, and the *personalist* interpretation, according to which basic probability statements essentially record the degree to which someone accepts some proposition or other. (PAFE, 14–15)

After examining whether the atheist's argument against God is cogent on any of these theories of probability, Plantinga concludes "that none of the main interpretations of probability provide the atheologian [i.e., atheist] with resources for a decent objection to theism" (PAFE, 47–48). In a later article in 1988, "Epistemic Probability and Evil" (EPAE), Plantinga develops the previous argument, and additionally considers whether a fourth theory of probability could help the atheist: "epistemic probability." (Answer: no.) Unfortunately, the details of these technical, though highly rewarding discussions, are simply outside the scope of this volume.

---

strategies is exposing atheist ignorance as relevant against the cogency of their own arguments. Of course, Plantinga's particular strategy here adapts his FWD, and so inherits any liabilities of that approach mentioned earlier.

Fourth Reply: Endorsing Skeptical Theism (1988, 2000, 2011)

Fourth, Plantinga has urged the "inscrutability defense" against the evidential problem of evil, developing it in great detail in several writings (especially in *WCB*, 458–98). On this view, while Rowe believes his "factual premise"—"There exist instances of pointless evil"—he doesn't have the right to believe it. The only basis Rowe gives for this claim is how things "appear" to him: it appears to him that an animal's suffering in the forest fire is pointless. Likewise for the particularly difficult cases of rape, abuse, and torture mentioned earlier—these appear pointless. But while we can agree with Rowe that these evils certainly look pointless, does that give us good reason to think they are pointless? Wouldn't God, if he existed, be omniscient and perfectly wise, and so know quite a bit more than we do about the role evils play in the unfolding of history and the bringing about of future goods? Wouldn't God know quite a bit more about the range of possible goods to be aimed at in providence, and the conditions of their realization, than we do? Wouldn't God, if he existed, be omnipotent and therefore able to realize very deep goods over time, in ways we cannot at present fathom? At any rate, what does Rowe or anyone else know that rules out (or makes unlikely) the idea that evils have a point? As Plantinga puts it,

> Suppose the fact is God has a reason for permitting a particular evil . . . , and suppose we try to figure out what that reason might be: is it likely that we would come up with the right answer? Is it even likely that we would wind up with plausible candidates for God's reason? . . . [There is an] epistemic distance between us and God: given that God *does* have a reason for permitting these evils, why think we would be the first to know? Given that he is omniscient and given our very substantial epistemic limitations, it isn't at all surprising that his reasons for some of what he does or permits completely escape us. (*WCB*, 466–67)

It is only rational to infer from an *appearance* of pointlessness to *genuine* pointlessness, if we are able to *tell the difference* between the two. But why should we puny, finite humans think that we can tell the difference? Perhaps the complexities of an infinite God's providential plan would not be immediately discernible by us (to put it mildly). Plantinga illustrates the real question like this:

> I look inside my tent: I don't see a St. Bernard; it is then probable that there is no St. Bernard in my tent. That is because if there were one there, I would very likely have seen it; it's not easy for a St. Bernard to avoid detection in a small tent. Again, I look inside my tent. I don't see any noseeums (very small midges with a bite out of all proportion to their size); this time it is not particularly probable that there are no noseeums in my tent—at least it isn't any more probable than before I looked. The reason, of course, is that even if there were noseeums there, I wouldn't see 'em; they're too small to see. And now the question is whether God's reasons, if any, for permitting such evils . . . are more like St. Bernards or more like noseeums. (*WCB*, 466)

Skeptical theism first rose to prominence in the contemporary era with Stephen Wykstra's 1984 article, "The Humean Objection to Evidential Arguments from Suffering: On Avoiding the Evils of 'Appearance.'"[12] Plantinga soon incorporated this style of reply in his own philosophical writing, starting with "Epistemic Probability and Evil" (1988) and continuing in *Warranted Christian Belief* (2000) and chapter 2 of *Where the Conflict Really Lies* (2011). Of particular interest is Plantinga's case that this approach dovetails quite nicely with explicit biblical themes about the inscrutability of God's purposes. He offers an extended exposition of many passages

12. Stephen J. Wykstra, "The Humean Objection to Evidential Arguments from Suffering: On Avoiding the Evils of 'Appearance,'" *International Journal for Philosophy of Religion*, 16, no. 2 (1984): 73–93.

in the book of Job that are exactly as one would expect if skeptical theism were the right way to think about evil (*WCB*, 494–98).[13]

Fifth Reply: Endorsing Supralapsarian Theodicy (2004)

Fifth, in "Supralapsarianism, or 'O Felix Culpa'" (SOFC), Plantinga endorses a "supralapsarian theodicy" according to which

> God wanted to create a highly eligible world, wanted to actualize one of the best of all the possible worlds; all those worlds contain atonement; hence they all contain sin and evil. . . . "Why does God permit evil?" The answer is: because he wanted to actualize a possible world whose value was greater than L; but all those possible worlds contain Incarnation and Atonement; hence all those worlds contain evil. So if a theodicy is an attempt to explain why God permits evil, what we have here is a theodicy—and, if I'm right, a successful theodicy. (SOFC, 373)[14]

Plantinga develops his argument over the course of twenty-five pages, so several elements of the above citation need explaining.

First, a longstanding dispute among Reformed Christians is whether God's decree to elect some to salvation is logically *prior* to (and therefore explanatory of) his decrees to create and to permit the fall, or whether the latter decrees are prior to the former. The first position is called "supralapsarianism," and the second is called "infralapsarianism." Plantinga thinks that it's easier to adjudicate this theological debate once we think about the problem of evil.

13. Just to be clear, "skeptical theism" isn't skeptical about *God*. On the contrary, the term "skeptical" refers to whether we should confidently infer that God doesn't exist simply because we can't discern his purpose in any case of evil. We should be skeptical *about such inferences*. They are dubious, given our finitude.

14. "L" is that level "of excellence or goodness" that "a highly eligible world" will have. See below.

And he argues that the best answer to that problem turns out to be the supralapsarian view. God first and foremost aimed at salvation realities (that there would be incarnation and atonement), and because of that he subsequently aimed at creation and fall, as a means to getting a world with incarnation and atonement.

Second, all possible worlds are very good worlds simply in virtue of the fact that God (a being of unlimited value) exists in each of them. On Plantinga's view, God exists in all possible worlds, and the value of God's existence will all by itself outweigh any creaturely evils in a world. So any possible world is an "eligible world," not excluded by God's goodness from being a candidate for creation. (We'll return to Plantinga's thoughts on God's "maximal greatness" in the next chapter.)

Third, God would want to do better than create a merely "eligible world"; he would want to create a "highly eligible" world. And "some possible worlds are much better than others" (SOFC, 370), namely those worlds that have "the towering and magnificent good of divine incarnation and atonement" (SOFC, 371). In fact, since the value of a world with incarnation and atonement is so great, it would be more valuable than any fallen world without incarnation and atonement, and indeed more valuable than any unfallen world without incarnation and atonement. A world with incarnation and atonement is the *most valuable* kind of world possible, and so God would aim at bringing about such a world.

Fourth, since "a necessary condition of atonement is sin and evil," it follows that "sin and evil is a necessary condition of the value of every really good possible world" (SOFC, 373). God permits sin and evil because he is aiming at the extraordinarily great value of salvation realities—incarnation and atonement. "God's ultimate aim . . . is to create a world of a certain level of value," and that "requires that there be sin and evil" (SOFC, 374).

Fifth, Plantinga counsels his readers to look at the problem of evil from the perspective of "Christian belief":

> Jesus Christ, the second person of the divine Trinity, incomparably good, holy, and sinless, was willing to empty himself, to take on our flesh and become incarnate, and to suffer and die so that we human beings can have life and be reconciled to the Father. In order to accomplish this, he was willing to undergo suffering of a depth and intensity we cannot so much as imagine, including even the shattering climax of being abandoned by God the Father himself: "My God, my God, why have you forsaken me?" God the Father, the first being of the whole universe, perfectly good and holy, all-powerful and all-knowing, was willing to permit his Son to undergo this suffering, and to undergo enormous suffering himself, in order to make it possible for us human beings to be reconciled to him. And this in face of the fact that we have turned our back upon God, have rejected him, are sunk in sin, indeed, are inclined to resent God and our neighbor. Could there be a display of love to rival this? More to the present purpose, could there be a good-making feature of a world to rival this? (SOFC, 368–69)

Sixth, Plantinga is here reversing his longstanding position that Christian theodicies are unsuccessful. He declared in his "Self-Profile" of 1985: "And here I must say that most attempts to explain *why* God permits evil—*theodicies,* as we may call them—strike me as tepid, shallow and ultimately frivolous" (SP, 35). But nearly twenty years later he ended up endorsing this "O felix culpa" theodicy as a serious theodicy for the problem of evil.[15]

Plantinga goes on to defend this theodicy against several objections, including the idea that this approach reveals God to be "unloving" and "unfair," and he supplements his presentation

15. As Plantinga points out, this Latin phrase comes from the liturgy for the Roman Catholic Easter Vigil: "O felix culpa, quae talem ac tantum meruit habere Redemptorem." Translation: O fortunate fault, which has merited such and so great a Redeemer!

with some of his earlier thinking on the problem of evil. As with his adaptation of Calvin's doctrine of the *sensus divinitatis* to matters of faith and reason (see the previous chapter), Plantinga's supralapsarian theodicy is yet another example of how distinctive Christian ideas from the past can impact the practice of Christian philosophy in the present.

4

PLANTINGA ON THEISTIC ARGUMENTS

Can we show by argument that there is a God? Have others shown by argument that there isn't a God? Whether there are any good theistic (or atheistic) arguments has occupied the attention of philosophers and theologians for at least 2,400 years. While Plantinga is a relatively recent contributor to this very old and extraordinarily complex discussion, his position is both significant and easily summarized: God's existence has not been disproved by argument, is rationally permissible to accept, and is supportable by way of argument.[1]

Plantinga's position is an interconnected whole, because the second point presupposes the first one (disproved beliefs can't be rational to accept), and the third point confirms the second one (a belief is all the more rational to accept if it can be supported

1. Given what we saw earlier in chapter 2, Plantinga's Reformed epistemology would add a fourth item to this list: God's existence doesn't need to be supported by any argument in order for belief in God to be justified, rational, and warranted, and to count as knowledge.

by argument). Nevertheless, his package of views falls short of what many Christians have traditionally believed on these topics. Whether that is a problem will be considered in chapter 7 (on Plantinga's philosophical method) and chapter 8 (on Plantinga and the Reformed heritage). While such evaluation is entirely appropriate, it will be misguided if the main contours of Plantinga's position are misunderstood. The rest of this chapter thus seeks to explain his three main points about theistic arguments: defeating the defeaters, rational permissibility, and natural theology.

Defeating the Defeaters: Belief in God Isn't Proved False by Argument

Whether or not belief in God is rationally permissible or likely to be true (points to be discussed later), Plantinga is convinced that no one has successfully disproved God's existence. This isn't for lack of trying on the part of atheists, of course. As we saw in chapter 1, Plantinga was exposed to a wide range of attempted disproofs of God's existence while in grad school (particularly at the University of Michigan). Most of these arguments he saw as question begging, that is, they assume what is to be proved. But all of them advertise themselves as "defeaters" for belief in God. Once you understand the argument and see its premises as likely to be true, you would also see that your belief in God can't be true, or in fact isn't true, or was very unlikely to be true, or (failing all of that) as lacking any kind of support. The reasoning allegedly exposes your faith in God as mistaken, unlikely, or blind. Such arguments are called defeaters because they are ways of defeating the acceptability of belief in God, at least for people who hope to be justified, rational, warranted, or otherwise intellectually proper in their beliefs.

As we saw in the last chapter on the problem of evil, there are two types of defeaters: undercutting and rebutting. An *undercutting* defeater argues that someone's belief lacks reasons or grounds—in the absence of this, he had better find some reasons or grounds if he's going to have a right to hold the belief. A *rebutting* defeater argues that someone's belief is false—so he had better eliminate it right away! In response to all such arguments, Plantinga has devoted a good bit of his career to "defeating the defeaters," to showing that these arguments against God don't work. His writing here falls into three categories.

The Problem of Evil

An initial rebutting defeater for God's existence is *the problem of evil.* The idea is that the existence, amount, or variety of evil in the world shows that God's existence is either impossible (the logical problem of evil) or very unlikely (the evidential problem of evil). We've already seen Plantinga's response to this defeater in the previous chapter, so there is no need to repeat that material here. But we can summarize his response by using the undercutting/rebutting distinction just explained. In response to the logical problem of evil, Plantinga offers both an undercutting defeater (Mackie's conclusion is inadequately supported) and a rebutting defeater (the free will defense proves that God and evil are consistent with each other, and therefore that Mackie's conclusion that evil contradicts the existence of God is false). And in response to the evidential problem of evil, Plantinga again can be seen as offering both an undercutting defeater (skeptical theism shows that the assumption of pointless evil is inadequately supported) and a rebutting defeater (supralapsarian theodicy shows that God does have a reason for permitting evil, contrary to those who say he doesn't).

The Incoherence of Theism

A second rebutting defeater for God's existence consists of so-called *incoherence of theism arguments.* These arguments seek to show that God can't exist because the very concept of God is incoherent, contradictory, or impossible to define. For instance, it is argued that there can't be an all-knowing (i.e., omniscient) being because such a being would have to know the set of all truths. But set theory implies that there can't be a set of all truths, and so there can't be an omniscient being. Or again, it is argued that there can't be an omniscient being who also creates free human beings like us, because no one can know ahead of time how humans will use their free will. Or it is argued that it's incoherent to claim that God exists, because if God is infinite or transcendent, then none of our concepts can apply to him. Since we have to know something about God in order to conclude that he exists, it follows that we can't conclude that he exists. Plantinga thinks that all such arguments are bogus, and we'll see his replies to these specific ones (and more) in chapter 5, when we look at Plantinga on the divine attributes.

Science vs. Religion

A third undercutting defeater for God's existence is the whole category of *science vs. religion arguments*. For example, the biological theory of evolution allows atheists to be "intellectually fulfilled" (Richard Dawkins's phrase), since evolution explains what previous generations thought only the existence of God could explain: the appearance of design. The doctrine of a creating, provident God is undercut, as it were, by the availability of a nontheistic explanation of any evidence for creation and providence. There is no need to believe in such a God anymore! Or again, contemporary physics can explain all motion and activity by the laws of nature, so there is no longer any need to believe in a God who actively sustains the world or miraculously acts within it. Or again, evolutionary psychology can explain why we have religious beliefs: they have survival value or are a side effect of that which has survival value. Being thus explainable, there is no longer any reason to think that religious beliefs are true. In chapter 6, we'll see how Plantinga responds to such arguments.

These defeaters are generated because their proponents assume that there is conflict between the existence of God and either (1) the existence of evil, (2) the dictates of reason, or (3) the deliverances of science. Plantinga's overall strategy to defeat such defeaters is to argue that the alleged conflict dissolves upon further scrutiny. Of course, there is no general way to defeat these arguments; you have to look at the details, and so different arguments deserve different replies. As a creation of God, the human mind is a very complicated thing, and fallen reason can generate a multitude of complex rationalizations for not believing in God. The fall of man is so bad that it even perverts and exploits God-given ingenuity, complicating the task of the Christian apologist. Still, our faith in God can be indirectly bolstered by seeing how many attempts to disprove God fail. God can make the wrath of man praise him (Psalm 76:10).

Rational Permissibility: Belief in God Is Proved Rationally Permissible by Argument

Plantinga, of course, thinks we can go much further than this when it comes to arguments for God. Not only do the arguments against God not work, but we can show by way of argument that it is entirely permissible to believe in God, given all the demands of rationality. Whether or not we can come up with an argument that shows that God exists, our believing in God certainly wouldn't go against rationality. (If God's existence could be disproved, then clearly belief in God would go against rationality; thus, the present point presupposes Plantinga is right about the earlier one.)

This second fundamental point, about the "rational permissibility" of belief in God, is easily misunderstood. The two arguments we're about to discuss aren't intended by Plantinga to show that God does exist. Rather, they're meant to show that belief in God is *no worse off* than many other rational beliefs we have. Plantinga thinks there is a double standard at work among many who dispute whether we have any good arguments for God. Such people demand arguments for God that start from premises accepted by everybody, and then when theists fail to supply such arguments, the critic declares belief in God to be irrational. Meanwhile, such critics are happy to accept as rational many beliefs that aren't supported by such arguments either!

The Parity Argument from Other Minds (1967)

The central argument of Plantinga's early book *God and Other Minds* (1967) is the following:

> Premise P1: "If my belief in other minds is rational, so is my belief in God."
>
> Premise P2: "But obviously the former [belief in other minds] is rational."
>
> Conclusion: "So, therefore, is the latter [my belief in God]." (*GOM*, 271)

Plantinga assumes that no critic of God will reject premise P2, since everyone accepts that the belief that other people exist is a rational belief. But what about premise P1? Why should one think that belief in other minds and belief in God have equivalent rationality? To support premise P1, Plantinga considers the teleological (or "design") argument for God's existence and compares its cogency with the argument for other minds. He concludes in chapter 4 that the best version of the design argument for God is an *analogical* argument, asserting an analogy between the universe and artifacts produced by human intelligence. By analogy, since the latter are designed, so is the former, and so the universe itself has a designer. But Plantinga highlights the eighteenth-century Enlightenment skeptic David Hume's critique of this analogical design argument and agrees with Hume that the argument suffers from a fundamental flaw: the analogical "evidence is altogether ambiguous" (*GOM*, 109).

The designers of human artifacts are very different from (or "disanalogous" to) the God who designed the world. Human artifacts are:

- Typically designed by multiple people, but there is just one God.
- Created using preexisting material, but God created from nothing.
- Typically created by someone other than the designer, but God both designed and created the world.
- Designed by those who are limited in knowledge, power, and goodness, but God is unlimited in these respects.
- Designed by designers who have bodies, but God is spirit.

Because the analogical argument for God transfers none of these features of human designers to God, when by the strict rules of analogy it ought to do so, it turns out to be a very weak argument. Paying attention only to the evidence, that evidence is just as strong against God as for him.

In chapters 8 and 9, Plantinga turns his attention to the analogical argument *for other minds*. How do I know that there are other people in addition to myself? After all, I don't experience the personhood of other human beings directly. Perhaps they're all cleverly disguised robots, or zombies with no interior mental life, rather than persons! Answer: because I know I am a person, and the other human beings around me behave and speak in ways that are similar to how I behave and speak. For instance, when I am in pain, I behave and speak in specific ways. So, by analogy, when other human beings behave and speak in the same ways, I can rationally infer that they are in pain, and therefore are persons.

Plantinga notes that this analogical argument is the best argument for the existence of other minds that philosophers have produced, and that it "strongly resembles the teleological argument for the existence of God. They answer similar questions;

both are inductive or analogical arguments; each is perhaps the most successful answer to the question it addresses" (*GOM*, 245). But the analogical argument is subject to the same criticism that Hume raised against the design argument for God (*GOM*, 252–53). For example, every instance of pain I feel:

- Is felt by me, but all other pains aren't felt by me.
- Is felt in my body, but all other pains don't occur in my body.
- Are accompanied by my pain behavior, but all other pains aren't accompanied by my pain behavior.
- Is only felt by me, but all other pains are felt by others.

So, what characterizes my pains is very different from what characterizes the pains of others. Thus, the analogy is *extremely weak*, and by the strict rules of analogy, the evidence of my pains is just as much an argument against the existence of other persons as for them.

And that means that premise P1 is true: belief in God is no less rational than belief in other minds, since the cases for both are very similar and yet equally flawed. But since belief in other minds is rational, so is belief in God. Plantinga has in effect pursued a triple analogy: (1) the analogy between the universe and human artifacts argues for the existence of a designer, (2) the analogy between my behavior and speech when in pain and the similar behavior and speech of others argues for the existence of other persons, and (3) the analogy between these two arguments shows that they are "on an epistemic par" because they suffer the same flaw: the existence of disanalogies, such as those listed above. From the perspective of rationality, belief in God is no worse off than belief that other people exist.

The Modal Ontological Argument (1974)

In *God and Other Minds* (1967), Plantinga evaluated the other traditional arguments for God's existence—the ontological and cosmological arguments—and concluded that they are even more flawed than the teleological argument. But in 1974, in *The Nature of Necessity* (*NN*) and *God, Freedom, and Evil* (*GFE*), Plantinga revisited the first of these arguments at length and offered a version which he said proved that belief in God is rational. Anselm of Canterbury's ontological argument for God's existence, set forth in his *Proslogion* (eleventh century), maintained that it was contradictory for anyone to conceive of God as a perfect being and yet deny his real existence. Anselm was intrigued by Psalm 14:1—"The fool says in his heart, 'There is no God'"—and thought that his ontological argument brought out more fully why the fool was indeed foolish. He has an *idea* of God ("in his heart"), but from that very idea one can conclude that God exists, contrary to what the fool thinks.

Anselm's argument was criticized by many, including Thomas Aquinas (thirteenth century) and Immanuel Kant (eighteenth century), but Plantinga thinks his "modal" version of the argument offered in 1974 escapes these criticisms. Assume that a maximally excellent being is omniscient (all-knowing), omnipotent (all-powerful), and perfectly good, and that a maximally great being has this maximal excellence in every possible world (in every possible situation, or "way things could be"). It follows that if such a maximally great being were to exist, then his nonexistence would have been impossible. (After all, if he exists, he exists in every possible world, by the definition of "maximal greatness.") But according to a widely accepted principle of modal logic—the logic that studies the properties of necessity and contingency—if something is impossible in any world, it is impossible in all worlds, since what is possible or impossible does not vary across possible worlds.[2] So, the nonexistence of the maximally great being would be impossible in the actual world as well (our world), and so he must exist. In

2. The widely accepted principle of modal logic is a formula of S5 modal logic: $\Diamond\Box p \supset \Box p$, or "if something is possibly necessary, then it is necessary." See *NN*, 51–52, or any standard textbook on modal logic, for details.

this way, Plantinga argued that if it is even possible for there to be a maximally great being, then there must be such a being.

This new version of the ontological argument stimulated much vigorous discussion. Plantinga is clear that the argument falls short of demonstrating that God must exist. Rather, it establishes the "rational acceptability" of theism because its initial premise—that "maximal greatness is possibly exemplified"—is merely rational to accept. On the one hand, we don't have any reason to think that there couldn't be a maximally great being; for instance, it's not a contradictory concept. But, on the other hand, "not everyone who understands and reflects on" this premise "will accept it." We can't show that maximal greatness is possible. Maybe it's not possible!

> Still, it is evident, I think, that there is nothing *contrary to reason* or *irrational* in accepting this premise. What I claim for this argument, therefore, is that it establishes, not the *truth* of theism, but its rational acceptability. (*GFE*, 112)

Like the earlier analogical argument for God, Plantinga's modal ontological argument only concludes that God's existence is as *rational* to believe as many other beliefs we have no reason to doubt (such as belief in other minds, or belief that maximal greatness is possible).

Natural Theology: Belief in God Is Supported by Argument

Plantinga doesn't think that we are restricted to merely "defeating the defeaters" or merely establishing the rational permissibility of believing in God. He also thinks that the truth of God's existence is supportable by way of argument. Early in his career, in *God and Other Minds* (1967), Plantinga vigorously and negatively evaluated the main three traditional arguments for God (Aquinas's cosmological argument, Anselm's ontological argument, and the teleological argument discussed by Hume). But he is clearly a fan of less developed, more intuitive theistic arguments, having explicitly endorsed the cogency of such arguments in multiple venues.

"Two Dozen (or so) Theistic Arguments" (1986)

First, Plantinga gave a lecture in 1986 that remained unpublished for at least twenty years, but was widely circulated in manuscript form: "Two Dozen (or so) Theistic Arguments" (TDOSTA). It is a kind of manifesto on behalf of natural theology, which is arguing for God from the evidence of nature. The length of each argument ranges from a few paragraphs to a few pages, and the breadth of the offered evidence for the existence of God is breathtaking, offering metaphysical, epistemological, moral, and aesthetic arguments:

Intentionality	Collections	Natural numbers
Counterfactuals	Physical constants	Naïve design argument
Kenny's design argument	Ontological argument	Contingent existence
Positive epistemic status	Reliable proper function	Simplicity
Induction	No global skepticism	Reference
Plus and quus	Intuition	Moral argument / evil
Colors and flavors	Love	Mozart
Play and enjoyment	Providence and miracles	Nostalgia
Meaning of life	Argument from A to Z	

The original lecture notes are less than twenty pages long. But Jerry Walls, one of Plantinga's graduate students in the 1980s, was so impressed with these argument sketches that he went on to edit (with Trent Dougherty) a 400-page anthology of essays, each of which rigorously expands upon one of the arguments above. The resulting volume has twenty-seven contributors, testifying to the excitement and interest in natural theology that Plantinga has generated.[3]

Nevertheless, it is important to clarify the nature of the support given to the claim that "God exists" by the various arguments endorsed by Plantinga. We can distinguish at least four possible kinds or degrees of support:

- ***Necessarily**, God must exist, and the contrary is simply impossible,* because God's existence is the very precondition of intelligibility, meaning, and predication (Cornelius Van Til's transcendental argument).
- *God **certainly** exists,* because his existence deductively follows from undoubtable premises (Thomas Aquinas's classic natural theology).
- *God **very likely** exists,* because inductive argument shows that he is the best explanation for a wide range of empirical data (Richard Swinburne's probabilistic natural theology).
- *There is **good reason** to believe that God exists,* at least more reason than we had before considering a particular theistic argument.

Plantinga never characterizes his theistic arguments as offering anything more than the fourth kind of support listed above. While we will return to this matter of degrees of support in chapter 7, suffice it to say that Plantinga thinks that the traditional standards to which "good theistic arguments" are held are "wholly unrealistic." Admittedly, "none starts from premisses that are self-evident (or even accepted by every reasonable person who considers them) and proceeds inexorably by self-evident argument forms to the conclusion that theism is true" (PFNT, 312). However, Plantinga

3. Jerry Walls and Trent Dougherty, eds., *Two Dozen (or so) Arguments for God: The Plantinga Project* (New York: Oxford University Press, 2018).

points out that very few things we believe are based on arguments as rigorous as that. Why hold natural theology to such a high standard, while giving a pass to the arguments of philosophy, science, and history? That's just another double standard foisted on us by our secular culture.

Let's say your friend claims to have just won the lottery, and the next day starts driving around in an expensive sports car. While his new car doesn't decisively prove his claim, it raises the likelihood that his claim is true. We can say that your observing his new Porsche confirms his claim, since his winning the lottery is a better explanation of his sudden acquisition of that car than any alternative explanation that comes to mind. Now perhaps no single observation of yours proves your friend won the lottery. But his new car provides good evidence for an argument that he won it—perhaps one of many good arguments you could give as you continue to reflect on the matter. Plantinga would say that it's impossible to quantify these relations of support; they seem to operate at an intuitive level. Nevertheless, theistic arguments that are like this are still good arguments, and they come from a multitude of sources. "They can serve to bolster and confirm ('helps' a la John Calvin); perhaps to convince" (TDOSTA, 461).

"Natural Theology" (1995) and "God, Arguments for the Existence of" (1998)

Second, in 1995 Plantinga wrote the entry for "Natural Theology" in *A Companion to Metaphysics* (NatT). While he doesn't actually *present* any theistic arguments there, he names fourteen different arguments that are a clear reference to his 1986 lecture. He again mentions his own standard for such arguments: they "can serve the function of strengthening and deepening belief in God and of moving people towards it" (NatT, 348). A few years later in 1998, Plantinga wrote the entry for "God, arguments for the existence of" in *The Routledge Encyclopedia of Philosophy*

(GAFE). Here he not only summarizes his criticisms of the cosmological, ontological, and teleological arguments, but also offers ingenious defenses of all three. Beyond that, Plantinga offers two versions of a moral argument for God's existence, and three more arguments for God from intentionality, sets, and appalling evil. (The latter all derive from the 1986 lecture.)

Where the Conflict Really Lies (2011)

Third and most recently, in *Where the Conflict Really Lies* (2011), Plantinga devotes nearly a third of the book to presenting both direct and indirect arguments for God, articulating and defending them in some detail. His two direct arguments are from the fine-tuning of cosmological constants (in the realm of physics), and from irreducible complexity (in the realm of biology). On fine-tuning:

> Astrophysicists and others have noted that several of the basic physical constants—the velocity of light, the strength of the gravitational force, and of the strong and weak nuclear forces—must fall within very narrow limits if intelligent life of our kind is to develop. . . . This seems to offer support for theism: given theism, fine-tuning is not at all improbable; given atheism, it is; therefore theism is to be preferred to atheism. (*WTCRL*, 194, 199)

Likewise in biology: "Vision, blood clotting, the transport of materials within cells, and the immune system . . . are a number of structures and phenomena at the molecular level that display 'irreducible complexity,'" where the latter is defined (following biochemist Michael Behe) as "a single system composed of several well-matched, interacting parts that contribute to the basic function, wherein the removal of any one of the parts causes the system to effectively cease functioning" (*WTCRL*, 225). While it seems impossible to explain such systems by way of step-by-step

Darwinian gradualism, they seem quite well explained by design (and therefore by a Designer).

Plantinga goes on to make a distinction between a *design argument* (which involves an inference from premises to conclusion) and *design discourse* (which involves a non-inferential, basic belief that arises in the context of a certain experience) (*WTCRL*, 240–48). On the latter, our simply being made aware of fine-tuning and irreducible complexity "puts us in the sorts of situations in which design beliefs are in fact formed" (*WTCRL*, 246), resulting in theistic beliefs less susceptible to defeat than if they had been based on inference. Still, Plantinga thinks that the fine-tuning and irreducible complexity data can be utilized in arguments for God, and as such "perhaps offer a certain limited but still non-negligible support for theism" (*WTCRL*, 265).

Beyond these two direct arguments for God, Plantinga's ten indirect arguments for God contend that theological truths account for many of the fundamental assumptions in science (*WTCRL*, ch. 9). That is, there is "deep concord" between religion and science, because the scientific worldview flourishes best in theological soil:

Theological truth		**Scientific assumption**
The doctrine of *divine creation*	accounts for	the reality and discoverability of the laws of nature, the status of these laws as both contingent and naturally necessary, the rationality of induction, and the importance of empirical investigation.
The doctrine of *divine providence*	accounts for	the stability and regularity of the world.
The doctrine of *divine ideas*	accounts for	the nature of numbers and sets, and our knowledge of mathematics.
The doctrine of *the imago dei* (our being created in the image of God)	accounts for	the match between our mind and the world, the applicability of mathematics to the world and its accessibility to us, and our reliable intellectual preference for simplicity.

The idea here is simple. Were it not for the doctrines in the left-hand column, the scientific assumptions in the right-hand column would have their feet firmly planted in midair. Scientific faith would lack a foundation, as it were. As Plantinga puts it:

> Theistic religion gives us reason to expect our cognitive capacities to match the world in such a way as to make modern science possible. Naturalism gives us no reason at all to expect this sort of match; from the point of view of naturalism, it would be an overwhelming piece of cosmic serendipity if there were such a match. (*WTCRL*, 303)

Plantinga has no interest in disputing the truths in the right-hand column. What he wants is an explanation for them, and he thinks he's found one in God.

5

PLANTINGA ON THE DIVINE ATTRIBUTES

The Coherence of Theism

As we saw in the previous chapter, in the section on "Defeating the Defeaters," one way to argue against the existence of God is to show that the very concept of God is self-contradictory or otherwise incoherent. Christians think that God's attributes all fit together and do not contradict each other, but the critics are here to argue otherwise. On this view, even as there are no square circles because there couldn't be a square circle, so there is no God because there couldn't be a God. The idea of God is just as self-contradictory as the idea of a square circle, or a married bachelor, or an immovable object encountering an irresistible force.

If successful, this would be a very good way of arguing against the existence of God. The critic doesn't have to get into the messy issue of weighing up empirical evidence for God (fine-tuning, irreducible complexity) and against God (evil). Rather, he can just restrict himself to examining concepts and seeing if they are compatible with each other. After all, we wouldn't bother trying to empirically examine the world to see if there are any square circles or married bachelors. We would already know from the start, by pure intellectual reflection, that there couldn't be such things.

But are the arguments for the incoherence of theism successful? The only way to find out is to deal with the alleged claims of incoherence one by one and show how the critic's arguments do not work. There's no need to view this enterprise as entirely negative, for it may very well be that the critic's attempt to argue against the coherence of theism becomes, in the providence of God, a means of strengthening the theist's faith. How? By addressing such arguments, theists have been forced to think through more deeply what they and other traditional theists really mean by the central claims of their faith, and deeper meditation on these claims can only do us good in the long run. They can help us to better articulate our theology, as we clarify what we mean by our terms. So we come through this whole process with a better understanding of our faith, thanks to the unwitting critic of our faith. God can work all things together for good (Romans 8:28), including intellectual opposition to the very idea of God.

In his philosophical work, Plantinga has devoted a significant amount of attention both to clarifying our talk of God's attributes and defending theistic doctrine from the claim that it is incoherent. In this chapter we will concern ourselves with three questions that Plantinga has addressed:

- Could God be metaphysically simple?
- Could there be an omniscient being?
- Could God's transcendence preclude our knowing anything about him?

Could God Be Metaphysically Simple?

Plantinga's Answer

Plantinga's only book-length foray into an examination of the divine attributes is the brief volume that contained his 1980 Aquinas Lecture at Marquette University: *Does God Have a Nature?* (*DGHAN*). Plantinga's working definition of God's "nature" is "a property he has essentially that includes each property essential to him" (*DGHAN*, 7). So, for instance, God's omniscience (all-knowingness) would be included in his nature, since God wouldn't be God if he failed to be omniscient (he would be a pagan runner-up for the title "God"). Omniscience is essential to him, as is omnipotence and perfect goodness, among many other properties that define God. But God's being the Creator isn't essential to him, and so it isn't part of his nature, since (presumably) he had the freedom to refrain from creating anything and thus the freedom not to be a creator. God would still be God—existing in eternal, self-sufficient, intra-Trinitarian fellowship—even if he hadn't created anything at all.[1]

Plantinga considers four answers to the question asked by the book's title: "Does God have a nature?" First, according to medieval theologian Thomas Aquinas's doctrine of divine simplicity, God has a nature, but he is identical to it. (Sound strange? See below.) Second, according to nominalists like the late medieval theologian William of Ockham, God doesn't have a nature, because there is no such thing as a nature, since there are no properties. Third, according to the "universal possibilism" of early modern philosopher René Descartes, God has no nature, not because there are no properties, but because while he has properties, he has no essential properties.

1. While God doesn't have to be a creator to be God, it is essential to God to be the creator of anything that exists, for nothing besides himself can exist except through his creative power. In addition, if God does decide to create, he only does so by virtue of what is included in his nature: his knowledge, power, goodness, etc.

Each of his properties could have been otherwise, because anything could have been otherwise (i.e., there is no necessity, and so no essences or natures). Plantinga critically evaluates each of these three answers—simplicity, nominalism, and universal possibilism—and rejects them. Instead, he offers a fourth answer: *God has a nature, but he is not identical to it.* Plantinga considers whether his answer denies God's sovereignty, since, if God's nature is distinct from him, then isn't who he is constrained by something that is not him? He also considers whether he should add to his view the idea that God sovereignly but necessarily creates his properties, and therefore creates his nature. (Answer: no.)

Approaching the issue as Plantinga does has a decidedly Christian apologetical bent, for he is seeking to steer his readers away from inadequate answers to the question, answers that offer incoherent theology to a watching world. While admitting that his own view invites "good questions, and good topics for further study" (*DGHAN*, 146), he is convinced that at the very least it is a consistent way of understanding how God relates to his nature, something not had by the other views.

The Rejection of Divine Simplicity

The entire book raises many extremely interesting issues, and it is additionally some of the clearest, most accessible material Plantinga has ever written. Critics might say that works against Plantinga, since on their view Plantinga's clarity reveals he is clearly wrong in some of his arguments and conclusions! In particular, by rejecting the first answer to the question, Plantinga ends up denying not only the truth, but also the very intelligibility of the traditional doctrine of divine simplicity (advocated by Augustine, Anselm, and Aquinas, and seemingly enshrined in the Westminster Confession, chapter 2.1, and the Belgic Confession, article 1). According to this doctrine, God is "simple," not composed; he therefore has no parts whatsoever, whether these be material parts (so, God is Spirit), temporal parts (so, God is timeless), or metaphysical parts (so, God is not composed of distinct properties). Plantinga argues that this doctrine of simplicity is incoherent and couldn't possibly be true, for it turns the thoroughly personal God into an impersonal abstract object, which is absurd.

But it turns out that Plantinga isn't really critiquing the traditional version of the doctrine at all. Broadly speaking, Plantinga is a Platonist in metaphysics, at least to the extent that he subscribes to a Platonic "one-*over*-many" understanding of universals (such as properties). Key to this view is the idea that concrete substances like rocks, trees, us, and God "exemplify" properties that exist distinct from the substances that exemplify them. This is often called a "relational" understanding of the metaphysics of properties—abstract properties stand in a relation of "exemplification" to the concrete substances which exemplify the properties. On this "*abstractionist*" view (the term is from philosopher Peter van Inwagen), abstract properties are distinct from concrete substances. There is the abstract property of humanity, and then there are us humans, who exemplify this property that is distinct from us. An alternative metaphysics is Aristotelian and "*concretist*," involving a "one-*in*-many" understanding of properties as concrete parts that compose concrete substances. The property of knowledge or justice, on this view, is a part (or constituent) of the things that are knowledgeable or just. Substances aren't related to externally and abstractly existing properties; they are (partly) constituted by their properties. For instance, if you were injured in a car crash, perhaps you would lose your degree of knowledge or power as a part of you, but you would persist. This mishap would reveal that these metaphysical parts are not essential to the particular being you are.

Although space does not permit a technical discussion, the difference between relational and compositional metaphysics may make a difference as to whether the doctrine of divine simplicity is intelligible, since that doctrine is simply (!) the thesis that God is without any parts whatsoever. For God, being knowledgeable isn't one of many divine parts that had to come together to compose the fullness of the divine being (with other parts being, say, justice, love, and power). Such a compositional view of God's being at least raises the question of how God came to be so composed, and of whether there is a more fundamental explanation of the fact that God is composed the way he is, rather than some other way. This is an eminently sensible question to raise about us humans and other creatures, since on most religious views our very nature depends on God's bringing into existence all of our metaphysical parts at once, when he brings us into existence. But the question of composition makes no sense at all when directed at God himself, and the doctrine of divine simplicity is there to ensure that nothing can explain God's metaphysical composition, since, unlike creatures, he isn't a composed being in any sense. Divine simplicity, then, is a safeguard against naive conceptions of the metaphysics of God that would be in considerable tension with the doctrines of divine ultimacy and self-sufficiency. Divine simplicity helps put the exclamation mark at the end of this sentence: There is no explanation—and there can't be any explanation—more ultimate than God himself, for why God is the way he is!

Bereft of this background in compositional metaphysics, and assuming a relational metaphysics instead, Plantinga would be right in *Does God Have a Nature?* that the doctrine of divine simplicity makes little sense. If properties were abstract, Platonic entities that are distinct from God, and which God exemplifies, then when the advocates of simplicity say that God is identical to his nature (his essential properties), they would have to be saying that God is the very abstract object which he exemplifies. And that does seem absurd. But if we instead assume a compositional metaphysics for creatures, then we can say that God by contrast is a simple being with no metaphysical parts. Rather, the entirety of who he is makes all the various claims about him true: that he is knowledgeable, just, powerful, etc. God is a concretely existing, personal being through and through, and the one simple thing he is makes true a whole range of diverse claims about him. There would be no need to conclude, as Plantinga forcefully does, that simplicity turns God into an abstract object.

The irony is that in other contexts, Plantinga clearly appreciates the Aristotelian perspective, such as when he tries to define "abstract object" in epistemological terms (*WPF*, 120–21). Perhaps *Does God Have a Nature?* is a theological discussion in which consulting the Aristotelian one-*in*-many perspective on properties could have deflected these well-intentioned but premature criticisms of a traditional doctrine about God.[2]

Could There Be an Omniscient Being?

When Plantinga reflects on our being created in the image of God, he often draws attention to the fact that God created us to be knowers. He says this in *WCB*, 188, when explaining why Christian belief is most likely warranted if true. If God exists and has created us, he would very likely want us to come to know him. And he says it in *WTCRL*, 4–5, 266–70, when explaining the value of science as a cooperative social enterprise in which we image God. It is no wonder, then, that the divine attribute

2. Plantinga seems aware of the compositional/relational distinction, but strangely says, "However, I think it is not significant" (*DGHAN*, 55). There are shrewd contemporary defenses of divine simplicity, such as the so-called truthmaker account of predication. See Michael Bergmann and Jeffrey E. Brower, "A Theistic Argument against Platonism (and in Support of Truthmakers and Divine Simplicity)," in *Oxford Studies in Metaphysics*, vol. 2, ed. Dean Zimmerman (New York: Oxford University Press, 2006), 357–86. Also see Jeffrey E. Brower, "Simplicity and Aseity," in *The Oxford Handbook of Philosophical Theology*, ed. Thomas Flint and Michael Rea (New York: Oxford University Press, 2011), 105–28. Of course, these defenses end up admitting that God himself may not have libertarian free will as Arminians commonly understand that idea. But presumably that wouldn't be a problem for the Reformed community!

that Plantinga has spent the most time articulating, applying, and defending in his philosophical work is omniscience. Two of Plantinga's most widely discussed writings on this divine attribute ask the following questions:

- Could God have foreknowledge while we remain free?
- Could God know everything despite various paradoxes about the infinite?

Could God Have Foreknowledge While We Remain Free? (1986)

The so-called free will / foreknowledge dilemma claims that if we have free will (able to do otherwise in the same exact circumstances), then God can't have foreknowledge of our free choices. Two key assumptions here are God's essential omniscience and the fixity of the past. According to the first assumption, God not only knows the future, but also couldn't fail to know the future in any respect. It is in the nature of God to know the truth on any topic, and so God couldn't be mistaken about what we do in the future. According to the second assumption (the fixity of the past), from where we are on the timeline right now, the past is over and done with. There's nothing I can do now to stop 9/11 from occurring (though perhaps there was something someone could have done back then to stop it). As Linda Zagzebski has put it, this is why we don't cry over spilt milk. There's nothing we can do about it.

Given these assumptions, God's foreknowledge of our future choices seems to be over and done with—it is in the past. Therefore, there's nothing I can do now to make that foreknowledge anything other than what it has been from all eternity. But then God's foreknowledge means I can't do otherwise than what God has always foreknown. So my freedom (at least on a widely accepted understanding of freedom) contradicts God's omniscience. This dilemma has been with us for well over two thousand years. The ancient Greeks debated secular versions of it (having to do with "fate" or "truth"), and early Christians such as Augustine inherited it as a live possibility because of their (correct) view that God is essentially omniscient and cannot err.

Plantinga doesn't respond to this dilemma by agreeing with the ancient Christian author Boethius that God is outside of time. In multiple places Plantinga says that divine timelessness is a mistake (*DGHAN*, 45–46; EPAE, 94n11). Nor does he respond by agreeing with compatibilists (Reformed or otherwise) that free will is compatible with determinism, and therefore with not being able to do otherwise. Nor does he respond by advocating open theism, according to which God simply doesn't know (at least not infallibly) what we will do. Rather, Plantinga goes Ockhamist.

In his 1986 paper "On Ockham's Way Out" (OWO), Plantinga revives the perspective of William of Ockham that God's foreknowledge was a kind of "soft fact" that wasn't subject to the fixity of the past. Therefore, we could do otherwise than as God always believed (even if we don't in fact do otherwise). However, Plantinga eschews any complicated attempt to distinguish between a soft fact and a hard fact in support of Ockham's view. Rather, he claims that we human beings have a "counterfactual power over the past." Take *p* to be a past fact, such as that Abraham once existed or the Peloponnesian War started in 431 BC. Plantinga thinks it is possible that I have the power to perform an action A, such that if I were to perform A, then *p* would have been false (OWO, 253, 257).

So, as a matter of fact, Abraham did exist four thousand years ago. But perhaps I have the power right now to give a lecture, write a book, or whatever, such that if I do that, then Abraham would never have existed. Similarly, God foreknows that I will freely type out the rest of this sentence. But perhaps I can do something right now (close my Word document?), and if I were to do that, then God would never have foreknown that I would finish the sentence (even if he actually does foreknow that, and has known it from all eternity). If so, then God's actual foreknowledge of what I will do is quite consistent with my ability to do otherwise.

To say that the discussion surrounding Ockhamism is both voluminous and complex would be a monumental understatement. Plantinga's article itself provoked much of the contemporary debate. Space permits three brief comments. First, as Plantinga admits, if what he says on p. 253 is correct, then "it is not easy to think of *any* contingent facts about the past that are accidentally necessary in that sense" (OWO, 257). Plantinga's view seems to eat away at our fundamental intuition about the fixity of the past, that the past deserves to be called "the past" because it is fixed. And that seems a high price to pay. If even the past existence of Abraham is up for grabs, as it were, then what is the difference between past and future? As Linda Zagzebski puts it, "The problem is that God's past beliefs seem to be as good a candidate for something that is strictly past as almost anything we can think of, such as an explosion last week." So how can "we have counterfactual power over God's past beliefs but not the past explosion"?[3]

Second, even if we have such a counterfactual power, could we ever exercise it? Presumably, at the time we exercise it, God's past belief about my choice has been a fact forever. So, if I were to exercise the power, then I would have to change that past fact into something else. Since that's absurd, then I can't in fact exercise this wondrous power, even if I have it. Partisans of free will won't be happy to learn that they "have" a power that can never in fact be exercised, given what the past has already been.

3. Linda Zagzebski, "Foreknowledge and Free Will," in *The Stanford Encyclopedia of Philosophy*, edited by Edward N. Zalta, Fall 2004 edition. https://plato.stanford.edu/archives/fall2004/entries/free-will-foreknowledge/. The quote is from §2.3, "The Ockhamist solution."

Third, when Plantinga explains the basis for this counterfactual power, he appeals to his Molinistic theory of divine providence, which is the idea that there are truths about how we would use our free will, and that God plans his universe by consulting such truths ahead of time: "It is possible that if God had foreseen that you would choose *that* alternative, he would have acted very differently. Perhaps he would have created different persons; perhaps, indeed, he would not have created Abraham" (OWO, 257). But if there are problems with Molinism, then Plantinga's Ockhamist approach might inherit them. (We considered his application of the Molinist idea to the problem of evil in chapter 3 and will consider its problems in chapter 8.)

Could God Know Everything Despite Various Paradoxes about the Infinite? (1993)

A deeper question now arrives on the horizon. Forget about whether God's omniscience is compatible with our free will. *Could* there even be an omniscient being at all? In the same year that Plantinga published the first two volumes of his trilogy on warrant (1993), he found time to publish a forty-page article debating coauthor Patrick Grim on the coherence of divine omniscience: "Truth, Omniscience, and Cantorian Arguments: An Exchange" (TOCA). Grim uses a "power set theorem" from the nineteenth-century German mathematician Georg Cantor to argue that there couldn't be a set of all truths. Imagine there are only three truths: {t1, t2, t3}. A being is omniscient if he knows all three. But wait a minute! Those can't be the only truths. There would also be truths about how many subsets of that set there are, and there seem to be six: {{t1}, {t2}, {t3}, {t1, t2}, {t1, t3}, {t2, t3}}. Well, OK, so God must know six more truths to be omniscient: the truth that {t1} is a subset of {t1, t2, t3}, the truth that {t2} is a subset as well, and so on. But then we can ask about that larger set of nine truths: isn't there a truth for each one of *its* subsets? The set of all truths continually gets bigger, and so Grim concludes: "For *any* set of truths T there will be some truth left out. There can be no set of all truths" (TOCA, 267). And that spells the end of divine omniscience: if there can't be a set of all truths, then there can't be a being who knows the set of all truths.

The ensuing exchange reveals the philosophical acumen of both authors, and the entirety of it can't be tracked here. But several of the salient moves offer insight into Plantinga's elegant apologetic strategy: clarify that a simple adjustment to the definition of omniscience avoids the paradox and point out that the opponent's position entails consequences he would not accept.

First, why assume that God's omniscience "demands that there be a *set* of all truths"? Rather, we can simply say that God "knows every true proposition and believes no false ones." God can "know all truths" without our having to understand that knowledge as knowledge of a set with members. At worst, we have "a difficulty, not for *omniscience* as such, but for one way of explicating omniscience, one way of saying what this maximal perfection with respect to knowledge is" (TOCA, 267–68, 291).

Second, if Grim is right that any quantification—such as "God knows every *x*"—must range over a set, then many everyday things Grim believes are thereby challenged. "There aren't any married bachelors" and "Everything is self-identical" are obvious truths, and they seem to be claims that range over the set of all things. But if there can't be a set of the latter, then these obvious truths are in trouble. Plantinga concludes: "These problems don't seem to me to have anything special to do with omniscience. . . . The problem won't be any worse in theology than anywhere else" (TOCA, 275).

Third, Plantinga says, "It seems to me that there is self-referential trouble with your position; it is in a certain way self-defeating. . . . It seems hard to see how to *state* your argument." Grim's conclusion, "There are no genuinely universal propositions," is itself a genuinely universal proposition! Likewise, at the end of the exchange, Plantinga notes that for any version of Grim's argument against omniscience, "its premises will *involve* quantification over all propositions," which is the very thing Grim's argument says can't be done. So, if Grim's argument "is sound, then there will be a sound argument against the existence of one of its premises: so it isn't sound" (TOCA, 285, 303, 305).[4]

Could God's Transcendence Preclude Our Knowing Anything about Him?

General Concerns

We've looked at divine simplicity and omniscience. What about God's transcendence and infinity? Some people think these preclude our finite human concepts from applying to God. That would spell disaster for our Christian beliefs, since beliefs involve concepts. You cannot believe that a chair is in the room unless you have a concept of a chair. You also predicate properties of the chair (size, color, stability). The same is true for belief in God, though of course the concepts and properties will be much different. But perhaps things go awry when we talk about the "omni" attributes of God. How can we limited beings cognitively grasp a being who has no limitations? Since the infinitude of God applies to all his attributes, every attribute of God generates this problem.

Plantinga devotes *DGHAN*, Part I, and *WCB*, chapters 1–2, to addressing this question. (The latter is an expansion of the former, with considerable overlap between the two presentations.) His most general reply is to argue that this kind of radical theological agnosticism is self-defeating. If "God is such that our concepts don't apply to him," then that statement is predicating a property

4. This move parallels the one we saw in chapter 2, that classical foundationalism in epistemology is self-referentially incoherent. We'll see the move yet again in the next section.

of God, and so at least some of our concepts do apply to him. So in "making a claim, they make a *false* claim." Likewise, perhaps critics are saying, "If there were an infinite, transcendent, and ultimate being, our concepts could not apply to it." But to make that claim, we have to have a concept of "infinite" (i.e., there are no limits to God's knowledge, power, etc.) and a concept of "transcendent" (God exists *a se* and is sovereign; he depends on nothing distinct from him, and everything distinct from him depends on him). But then the claim is: if a being is infinite and transcendent, then our concepts of infinity and transcendence don't apply to it. But in that case, why call the being infinite and transcendent in the first place (*WCB*, 6)?

Replies to Kant and Hick

Beyond these general concerns, Plantinga interacts with three authors often associated with this kind of radical theological agnosticism: the eighteenth-century Prussian philosopher Immanuel Kant, and the twentieth-century philosophers of religion Gordon Kaufman and John Hick.

On one plausible and popular reading, Kant holds that we can only know the *phenomena* (how things appear to us), and never the *noumena* (how things are in themselves). And that's because we can only *experience* the phenomena, not the noumena: "Everything intuited in space or time, and therefore all objects of any experience possible to us, are nothing but appearances, that is, mere representations" (*WCB*, 11, citing Kant's *Critique of Pure Reason*). Therefore, since our experience is limited to objects in space and time, we can have no knowledge of a God who exists outside of space and time. Plantinga thinks this position is subject to at least three replies.

First, Kant seems to be inconsistent, since he claims some knowledge about the noumena. For instance, he says that the noumena *cause experience* in us. Of course, the experience has no structure, so we then apply our categories and concepts to this experience, and thereby construct the phenomena. So our concepts do not apply to noumena, and are rather rules for constructing phenomenal objects out of the manifold of experience. Why then should we think that the noumena cause anything at all, much less all of our experience?

> (On this picture, we might say, Kant's thought founders on the fact that the picture requires that he have knowledge the picture denies him.) If this picture were really correct, the noumena would have to drop out altogether, so that all that there is is what has been structured or made by us. The idea that there might be reality beyond what we ourselves have constructed out of experience would not be so much as thinkable. (*WCB*, 20)[5]

Second, not only is Kant's view self-defeating; his arguments for his view are also self-defeating. His main reason for thinking that our concepts do not apply to noumena are the pro and con arguments he calls "antinomies." When we reason about things in themselves (the noumena), we can prove by pure reason that contradictory claims are both true. For instance, we can prove the "thesis" that the world has a beginning, and also prove the "antithesis" that the world does not have a beginning. This shows that we can't reason about the noumena successfully, since we end up in contradictions. So our concepts do not apply to it. Plantinga makes a shrewd reply: if Kant's antinomies are good arguments, then we can make them about the phenomena, and similarly end up in contradiction: the world appears to have a beginning, and appears not to have a beginning. When we reason about appearances, we end up in contradiction too. So, given Kant's argument,

5. Plantinga argues that similar self-referential problems apply to Gordon Kaufman's distinction between the "real referent" and the "available referent" (*WCB*, 38).

we can't think about the noumena or the phenomena. We can't think about anything (*WCB*, 23–24)!

Third, in any event, the antinomies just aren't good arguments, and so give us no reason for doubting that we can refer to, apply concepts to, or have knowledge of the noumena. Kant's argument for the antithesis, that the world does not have a beginning, assumes that "since the beginning is an existence which is preceded by a time in which the thing is not, there must have been a preceding time in which the world was not" (*WCB*, 25–26, citing Kant's *Critique*). But that unduly restricts the options. Following Augustine, perhaps the first moment of the universe was the first moment *of* time, and not merely the first moment of existence *in* time. Given this definition of the beginning of the universe, the question of what happened in the time "before" the universe is conceptually malformed. (It is like asking, "What point is north of the North Pole?" Given what we mean by "North Pole," every point on the globe is south of the North Pole, and necessarily so.)[6]

Plantinga raises further, very interesting questions about the radical theological agnosticism of the other authors. For instance, according to John Hick, there is a religiously Real ultimate behind all the world's religions, though none of our positive or substantial concepts apply to it (*WCB*, 46). But then, Plantinga asks,

> What reason is there for thinking this being is connected in some way with Christianity or with any other religion? Why say that Christians are in fact referring to or witnessing to this being? Maybe it is, instead, connected with warfare, prostitution, family violence, bigotry, or racism. And why think this being, or contact with it, has anything to do with "transformation of human existence from self-centredness to Reality-centredness"? (*WCB*, 56)

6. Cf. Augustine, *City of God*, trans. Henry Bettenson (New York: Penguin Books, 2003), xi. 6, p. 436: "The world was not created *in* time but *with* time. . . . At the time of creation there could have been no past."

The preceding has been just a taste of the kind of defenses Plantinga has offered for the possibility of the existence and knowability of God, against arguments to the contrary. There remains further work to be done, however. If arguments from reason alone don't show that belief in God is contradictory or otherwise undermined, then perhaps arguments from the deliverances of science do this. The next chapter surveys Plantinga's thought in response to this challenge.

6

PLANTINGA ON RELIGION AND SCIENCE

In chapter 4 on "Theistic Arguments," we saw Plantinga's twofold argument for concord between science and religion: irreducible complexity (in biology) and fine-tuning (in physics) directly support God's existence, and the availability of theological accounts for many of the presuppositions of science indirectly supports God's existence. But what about conflict between science and religion? Do contemporary biology or physics give us any reason to think that God hasn't created us, doesn't providentially sustain us, or can't directly act in the world? Does evolutionary psychology supply a reason to think that Christian belief is irrational or false? Many have alleged a conflict between these three sciences and the Christian faith, but is there actual conflict?

Throughout his philosophical career, Plantinga has answered no to all these questions—the conflict is either merely alleged but nonexistent, or is superficial at best. In addition, on his view, there is a conflict between science and religion, but not the one that is widely advertised in our increasingly secular culture: a deep conflict between science and the quasi-religion of naturalism. (The latter is the metaphysical view, not derivable from science itself, that the space-time continuum is all there is.) This is Plantinga's "naturalism defeated" argument, developed and refined over the course of almost twenty years. This chapter surveys Plantinga's attempts to both defuse any alleged conflict between science and religion and generate an actual conflict between science and quasi-religion, drawing primarily upon his most recent treatment of these issues in *Where the Conflict Really Lies* (2011). A common theme in Plantinga's writings on science is the idea that conflicts are needlessly generated between science and religion, and science as a knowledge discipline is needlessly undermined—by the gratuitous addition of nonscientific, naturalistic metaphysics to science.

Does Biological Evolution Undermine the Doctrine of Divine Creation?

Does biological evolution undermine the idea that God intentionally created us? According to Plantinga, it does only if we insist on a particular metaphysic that is not a deliverance of modern science: unguided natural selection (*WTCRL*, chs. 1–2). To see why Plantinga thinks that unguided natural selection would be central to establishing an incompatibility between biology and divine creation, we need to carefully define *evolution*, and then see the place of "unguided natural selection" within it.

Defining Evolution

Plantinga defines *evolution* using six theses that capture most of the ideas that evolutionists have in mind (*WTCRL*, 8–10):

1. The *ancient earth* is perhaps 4.5 billion years old.
2. There is a *progression* of life "from relatively simple to relatively complex forms."

3. *Descent with modification* produces diversity via offspring differing from their parents.
4. All life has a *common ancestry*; "life originated at only one place on earth . . . we are all cousins of each other."
5. Diversity is produced by a *naturalistic mechanism*: "natural selection operating on random genetic mutation."
6. Life had a *naturalistic origin* from nonlife.

Plantinga calls theses 1–4 "evolution" proper, whereas thesis 5 is "Darwinism," or the mechanism by which evolution is supposed to work.[1] This taxonomy is significant because it clarifies how we go about answering any charge of conflict between science and religion when it comes to evolution. With respect to theses 1–4, the conflict is generated by comparing a literal interpretation of Genesis with any one of these four claims. Once we see this, there are strategies to alleviate the conflict. As an example, Plantinga considers thesis 1. We could eliminate the conflict by appealing to the idea of "apparent age," thereby falsifying thesis 1. On this view, the earth looks ancient but isn't, because it was created a relatively short time ago with "crumbling mountains," fossils, starlight already in transit to earth, etc. Alternatively, we could eliminate the conflict by appealing to a nonliteral usage of "day" in Genesis 1, thereby accommodating thesis 1. (Similarly, we could posit a gap between Genesis 1:1 and 1:2, an option Plantinga doesn't mention.) Different believers would take different approaches, depending on their hermeneutical commitments.

Unfortunately, Plantinga doesn't offer much insight about how Christians might handle conflict generated by theses 2–4, though presumably here again Christians have the choice to *falsify* these claims (perhaps through appeal to intelligent design

1. Plantinga ultimately concludes that thesis 6 "isn't really part of the theory of evolution" (*WTCRL*, 10), and, as we saw in chapter 4, he thinks the evidence of irreducible complexity and fine-tuning stands against any naturalistic theory of origins.

or creation science) or *accommodate* them (perhaps by reconsidering one's interpretation of Genesis 1). Plantinga seems to hint at the latter strategy, as he approvingly quotes the Reformed theologian Charles Hodge to the effect that God's intentional creation of something is compatible with 1–4: "If God made them [plants and animals], it makes no difference how He made them, as far as the question of design is concerned, whether at once or by a process of evolution" (Hodge, in *WTCRL*, 11). One might think, then, that Plantinga is most naturally aligned with "theistic evolutionists," who accept theses 1–4, as contrasted with "old earth creationists," who only accept theses 1–2, and "young earth creationists," who accept none of the theses. But Plantinga has elsewhere argued that thesis 4 is unlikely to be true, given theism and the empirical evidence (ORTCA). So, his considered view seems to be that while theistic evolution (theses 1–4) is unlikely, its truth would be compatible with Christianity and therefore generate no conflict for it. (Compare this: I think it's unlikely that there are aliens on Mars, but their existence would be consistent with my religious beliefs.)

Defining Random

However, things are different with thesis 5. Whether or not "natural selection operating on random genetic mutation" excludes God's intentional creation of us depends on what we mean by "random." On some definitions of *random*, there is no conflict at all between random genetic mutation and God's intentional creation of us. For example, if "random" means "no correlation between the mutation and its utility for the organism"—which is what biologist Ernst Mayr and philosopher of biology Elliott Sober seem to have in mind—then this does not exclude intentional divine creation. God might bring about the mutation, but not because it has utility *for that organism*. Rather, he brings it about for *other* purposes, perhaps long-range ones. Clearly, God could bring about such a mutation directly, even if it were "random" in this sense. Or if *random* means "without a sufficient *physical* cause," because (say) mutations conform to probabilistic laws governing quantum phenomena, then this doesn't exclude intentional divine creation either. After all, God is a *nonphysical* cause, and he can nonphysically cause events that lack a sufficient physical cause (like mutations).

Of course, on some other definitions of *random* there is conflict between random genetic mutation and God's intentional creation of us. If *random* means "unguided by a personal agent"—which seems to be what evolutionists Stephen J. Gould, George Gaylord Simpson, and Richard Dawkins have in mind—then this would conflict with intentional divine creation. But no well-confirmed scientific theory supports the view that there are any random mutations in this sense. How could science prove that God didn't bring about a mutation for his purposes? Likewise, if *random* means "without any cause (physical or nonphysical)," then this obviously precludes God's causing random mutations. But how could science prove that God didn't cause a mutation? That would turn genetics into a theological theory: no nonphysical causes allowed!

It turns out that the only scientifically supportable ways of understanding thesis 5 are quite compatible with intentional divine creation, whereas interpretations of thesis 5 that conflict with intentional divine creation have nothing to do with science. Such interpretations employ the word *random* to mean "unguided" or "uncaused," making the thesis a nonscientific, metaphysical addition to the theory of evolution. For Plantinga, this is "where the conflict really lies": natural science gets confused with natural*ism,* which may indeed generate a philosophical conflict with religion, but not a scientific one. Plantinga concludes that a key source of alleged conflict between science and religion in the realm of biology is *the failure to detach naturalism from evolution.* It occurs when evolutionists insist, quite independently of any scientific evidence, that natural selection must be unguided.[2]

Does Physics Undermine the Doctrines of Divine Providence and Miracle?

Does the science of physics (whether classical or contemporary) undermine the idea that God acts in nature, providentially or miraculously? According to Plantinga, it does so only if we insist on a particular metaphysic that is not a deliverance of contemporary science: physical determinism, and the causal closure of the physical (*WTCRL*, chs. 3–4). To show that these philosophical concepts must be *added* to science to generate any conflict between physics and divine providence, Plantinga reflects on three theories of "the truth of physics" that have arisen in the history of science: Newtonian mechanics, Laplacean determinism, and quantum mechanics.

First, according to *Newtonian mechanics*, the behavior of matter in motion is subject to the general laws that the seventeenth-century English mathematician and physicist Isaac Newton famously discovered and published in his *Philosophiæ Naturalis Principia Mathematica* (1687), or "Mathematical Principles of Natural Philosophy." For instance, Newton's second law says that the force applied to a body is proportional to its acceleration and mass ($F = ma$), while his law of universal gravitation says that the gravitational force existing between two objects is proportional to their masses and inversely proportional to the square of the distances between them ($F = Gm_1m_2/r^2$).

2. Could there be a scientific case that natural selection is unguided by any intentional agent? Plantinga examines Richard Dawkins's case in detail and concludes that "what he shows, at best, is that it's epistemically possible that it's biologically possible that life came to be without design. But that's a little short of what he claims to show" (*WTCRL*, 25). The subtitle of Dawkins's *The Blind Watchmaker* is how "the evidence of evolution *reveals* a universe without design" (emphasis added), but Dawkins only offers a series of "feelings and guesses" in support of this grandiose claim (*WTCRL*, 22).

Some have thought that if these laws hold universally, then no one (not even God) could break them. Physical laws that can be broken are not really laws. So, if these laws hold, there is no need to appeal to God to explain motion in the world; indeed, it follows that God couldn't act in the world. On this view, Newton revealed that the universe is akin to a "machine" that is subject to no outside intervention. But Plantinga argues that this is an absurd understanding of Newton's contributions, for two reasons. First, Newton himself was a theist who "believed that God providentially guides the world. He also believed that God regularly adjusts the orbits of the planets; according to his calculations, their orbits would otherwise spiral off into chaos" (*WTCRL*, 77). He certainly never intended for his laws to be understood as requiring a kind of physical determinism that excluded God. Second, Newton's laws are widely understood as applying to closed systems. If nothing affects the physical system from the outside, then $F=ma$, $F = Gm_1m_2/r^2$, momentum is conserved, and so on. But if something does affect the physical system from the outside, then the system is open and all bets are off as to whether the law will accurately predict what will happen, given initial conditions:

> It is entirely possible for God to create a full-grown horse in the middle of Times Square without violating the principle of conservation of energy. That is because the systems including the horse would not be closed or isolated. For that very reason, there would be no violation of the principle of conservation of energy, which says only that energy is conserved in closed or causally isolated systems—ones not subject to any outside causal influence. It says nothing at all about conservation of energy in systems that are *not* closed; and, of course, if God created a horse *ex nihilo* in Times Square, no system containing that horse, including the whole of the material universe, would be closed. (*WTCRL*, 79)

This is why, when I subsequently catch a pencil that I have just released with my hand, thereby stopping its motion, I have not violated Newton's second law of motion. Rather, I have revealed that the pencil is in an open system, and so the law does not apply. For the same reason, God's directly acting in the world wouldn't break Newton's laws either. There is no conflict between physics and divine providence here.

Second, according to *Laplacean determinism,* it is not only the case that Newton's laws hold (along with all subsequently discovered physical laws), but also that the universe is physically determined and physically closed. Since it is determined, any earlier state of the universe—combined with the laws governing it—will entail any later state. And since it is closed, there couldn't be any intervention from outside the physical universe. The French mathematician and physicist Pierre Laplace (born a century after Newton) vividly described a "calculating demon" who, knowing the state of the universe at any point in time and all the laws of physics, would be able to deduce the state of the universe at any other point in time, whether past or future (*WTCRL,* 84). Here, Plantinga accepts the obvious: Laplace's picture of physics would conflict with divine providence and miracle. But it is just as obvious that Laplace's assumptions of determinism and closure have nothing to do with science. They aren't empirical discoveries about the world, and it is hard to see how they could be. Rather, as with the "unguided natural selection" touted by some biologists, Laplace's assumptions are a bit of metaphysics added to science. Again, there is no conflict between physics and providence here.

Finally, according to the twentieth-century development of *quantum mechanics,* the universe is subject to probabilistic laws that specify a "probability distribution" for any particular subatomic, quantum event. For instance, perhaps the laws say that a radium atom has a 33% chance of decaying in the next hundred years. But if that's how it is, then "Quantum mechanics offers *even less* of a problem for divine special action than classical science" (*WTCRL*, 91). Since quantum mechanics "doesn't determine a specific outcome for a given set of initial conditions, but instead merely assigns probabilities to the possible outcomes," then "special divine action, including miracles, is by no means incompatible with QM" (*WTCRL*, 94). In addition, perhaps quantum mechanics is right that there is no sufficient physical cause for any quantum event. Solely physical facts leave the outcome indeterminate. Still, it wouldn't follow in the slightest that there is no nonphysical cause for the event, such as God himself. In fact, Plantinga ingeniously argues that it is quite compatible with all discovered quantum laws that God could be directly causing all collapses of the "probability wave" into whatever quantum event he wants to bring about. According to his model of "divine collapse-causation," "between collapses, a system evolves according to the Schrödinger equation; but when a collapse occurs, it is divine agency that causes the specific collapse-outcome that ensues" (*WTCRL*, 116). There is no conflict between physics and providence here either.

Does Evolutionary Psychology Undermine the Truth of Christian Belief?

Does the science of evolutionary psychology undermine the idea that our deeply held religious beliefs are true? According to Plantinga, it does only if we insist on a particular metaphysic that is not a deliverance of contemporary science: that *the mechanisms for religious belief production are not truth-aimed* (*WTCRL*, ch. 5). Plantinga thinks that an examination of the typical evolutionary psychological explanations of moral and religious belief will reveal this hidden assumption.

Evolution says that creatures whose genes equip them or their group to survive will live longer on average than any peers without such genes, which means more of them will reproduce and so their genes will tend to predominate over time in the population. Natural selection will similarly operate on their offspring via their genetic endowment from their parents, exploiting any selective advantage that any random mutations might offer to them. Evolutionary psychology seeks to provide evolutionary explanations for distinctively human traits, such as belief and belief-based behavior. Because natural selection favors adaptive behavior, and therefore the traits that contribute to it, evolutionary explanations of moral and religious belief typically appeal to "functional" traits that promote survival or to "spandrel" traits that don't promote survival (being rather byproducts of what promotes survival).

Functional theories argue that the disposition to form various moral or religious beliefs contributes to the survival of the individual or the group, and it is for that reason that such dispositions were selected by natural selection. For instance, a functional theory of moral belief (Michael Ruse and E. O. Wilson, "The Evolution of Ethics" [1993]) assumes that cooperation among organisms will promote group survival, and that individuals with common moral intuitions are more likely to cooperate. So evolution will favor individuals with the following two moral beliefs: (1) there are objective obligations, and (2) the Golden Rule is one of these objective obligations. Belief in the Golden Rule is "a trick played on us by our genes to get us to cooperate," rather than one among many "objective moral obligations or requirements" (*WTCRL*, 134).

A "spandrel" theory of religious belief (Rodney Stark, *The Rise of Christianity* [1996]) assumes that our capacity for rational thinking—for figuring out which existing means are best suited to obtain our desired ends—promotes survival. So, evolution has hardwired in us a tendency toward rational, means-ends thinking. But, as a kind of side effect of this adaptive trait, we proceed to apply our capacity for rational thinking to *nonexistent* ends, thinking that praying or service is a means to get eternal life or salvation.

There is nothing adaptive about these religious beliefs—they don't help us to survive—but our tendency to form them is an unintended byproduct of a trait that is adaptive. Religion ends up being a kind of pseudo-answer to a pseudo-problem, exploiting our penchant for thinking rationally about economic exchange for goods, but here the exchange is between people and imagined supernatural agents for nonexistent goods.

Plantinga examines several such theories. He quotes Scott Atran (*In Gods We Trust* [2002]) as saying that "religion is (1) a community's costly and hard-to-fake commitment (2) to a counterfactual and counterintuitive world of supernatural agents (3) who master people's existential anxieties such as death and deception" (*WTCRL*, 139). According to D. S. Wilson (*Darwin's Cathedral* [2002]), "religion arises or at least becomes ubiquitous among human beings by way of group selection, because it is a useful form of social control that involves beliefs of a certain kind" (*WTCRL*, 143). According to Freud, religious belief is produced by wish-fulfillment: "The function or purpose of religious belief is really to enable believers to carry on in this cold and hostile or at any rate indifferent world in which we find ourselves" (*WTCRL*, 148). What all such theories have in common is the assumption that the moral obligations do not exist, the religious ends aimed at do not exist, and that the religious beliefs useful for social control or mastering anxieties or death are not true. But Plantinga asks: why make that assumption part of these theories? What empirical data tell us that the various moral claims or religious beliefs aren't true? Indeed, we could make all these theories simpler by subtracting these gratuitous assumptions of nonexistence and falsehood, and the theories would be just as empirically successful (to the extent that they make empirical predictions at all), but now they would be consistent with the truth of religious belief.

In the end, appealing to evolutionary psychology to generate a conflict with religion comes close to what logic textbooks call the "genetic fallacy": confusing the origin of a belief with its value. Plantinga explains:

> Describing the origin of religious belief and the cognitive mechanisms involved does nothing, so far, to impugn its truth. No one thinks describing the mechanisms involved in perception impugns the truth of perceptual beliefs; why should one think things are different with respect to religion? According to Christian belief, God has created us in such a way that we can know and be in fellowship with him. He could have done this in many ways; for example, he could have brought it about that our cognitive faculties evolve by natural selection, and evolve in such a way that it is natural for us to form beliefs about the supernatural in general and God himself in particular. Finding a "natural" origin for religion in no way discredits it. (*WTCRL*, 140)[3]

Does Naturalism Undermine the Scientific Enterprise?

Plantinga is also known for his "naturalism defeated" argument, developed over the course of twenty years:

- 1991: "An Evolutionary Argument against Naturalism" (AEAAN)
- 1993: "Is Naturalism Irrational?" (in *WPF*)
- 2000: "Naturalism and Lack of Knowledge" (in *WCB*)
- 2002: "The Evolutionary Argument against Naturalism" (EAAN)

3. Notice that here Plantinga is applying the fundamental insight derived from his "proper function" epistemology that we considered in chapter 2: knowledge crucially depends on how God made us to function, and discerning that takes us beyond what science and even epistemology are equipped to deliver. It takes us to metaphysics and even theology.

- 2008: "Against Naturalism" (ANat)
- 2011: "The Evolutionary Argument against Naturalism" (in *WTCRL*)

According to metaphysical naturalism, the space-time continuum is all there is; there is no such person as God or anything like God. So, if metaphysical naturalism were true and evolution produced us, then we would be the products of a blind, purposeless, unguided process that merely favors the preservation of all and only those genetic mutations that enhance survival. Creatures who outcompete their peers in the matter of feeding themselves, fleeing predators, and fighting predators (if they can't flee) will thereby live long enough to reproduce at a greater rate than their peers, thus bequeathing their superior genetic endowment to the next generation for preservation and further improvement by this same process. Whether or not their genetics additionally supply them with true beliefs (inner mental states that accurately represent their environment) is wholly irrelevant to the process of evolution. Maybe they do, maybe they don't—it is survival that matters. (Indeed, as we have seen, evolutionary psychologists who offer functional theories of religious belief are already committed to the view that false beliefs can have survival value.)

If Plantinga is right, then, while naturalism and evolution might make it highly likely that there would be creatures who successfully adapt to their environment, the likelihood of such creatures having true beliefs would be low. So, if you came to believe in naturalism and evolution, and furthermore saw that your cognitive reliability would be low if you were produced by naturalistic evolution, that would give you a reason to think that you likely don't have true beliefs, and this would extend to your belief in naturalism and evolution itself. In short, belief in naturalism and evolution gives you a good reason to abandon belief in naturalism and evolution. It is an intellectually self-defeating position.

Plantinga offers an analogy. If you came to believe that you had imbibed a drug ("XX") that inhibited cognitive reliability, so that any belief produced under the influence of that drug would be just as likely to be false as true, then you would cease to trust your cognitive faculties, for you would realize that your beliefs are being produced by a process that *isn't aimed at truth*. Believing in naturalism and evolution is like coming to believe that you have taken XX (*WTCRL*, 342). This line of reasoning isn't wholly original to Plantinga, for he cites correspondence in which Darwin himself apparently had doubts as to whether we should trust the deliverances of cognitive faculties that have been produced by a blind, purposeless process:

> With me, the horrid doubt always arises whether the convictions of man's mind, which has been developed from the mind of the lower animals, are of any value or at all trustworthy. Would any one trust in the convictions of a monkey's mind, if there are any convictions in such a mind? (Charles Darwin to William Graham, July 3, 1881, cited in *WTCRL*, 316)

Another analogy: when the engine of a locomotive burns coal, it causes the car to move forward. Of course, that same engine also causes smoke to emanate from the smokestack. But whether or not smoke gets produced makes no difference to whether the locomotive moves forward. Maybe there's smoke, maybe there isn't—what matters is the burning of the coal and the energy for motion it produces. Likewise, all that's required for survival value is that our neural states cause adaptive behavior. Yes, "this neurology also determines belief content, but whether or not that content is *true* makes no difference to fitness" (*WTCRL*, 327).

Since what evolution cares about is survival, not truth, it follows that naturalistic evolution is a worldview that comes apart at the seams: a naturalist who accepts evolution has good reason to doubt all his beliefs, including his belief in naturalistic evolution. It is important to clarify that Plantinga is certainly not contending for the absurd claim that our cognitive faculties aren't reliable! Rather, taking their reliability for granted, he is asking: on which view of the world does it make sense that we ended up with reliable cognitive faculties that produce mainly true beliefs via perception, memory, introspection, inference, and so on? If naturalistic evolution is true, then it is through sheer luck that we have our wondrous capacity for knowledge. But if God intentionally created us in his image (whether instantaneously or through a process of evolution that he guides), then he had good reason to create us to be knowers like him. Belief in God would enhance, rather than defeat, belief in our own cognitive reliability.

An obvious objection to Plantinga's argument is that we surely need true beliefs to survive, and so evolution would select for our survival by selecting ever more accurate capacities to believe the truth. But Plantinga argues that there is simply no reason to believe this. Many false beliefs would lead to survival as well. A vast number of variations on the following three kinds of examples could be provided (and Plantinga provides many). First, belief in false scientific theories can be pragmatically useful. Ptolemaic, geocentric astronomy—which says that the sun and stars revolve around an immovable earth—is quite useful even today to navigate the oceans of the world, despite being a literally false theory. Second, if Paul the caveman wants to be eaten by a tiger, but believes that the tiger in front of him doesn't want to eat him, this combination of desire and false belief will lead to adaptive behavior—Paul runs away (presumably to find a tiger he believes will want to eat him). Third, if someone has the false belief that everything is a witch, then the false belief that "This tiger-witch is dangerous" is nevertheless useful in leading to the adaptive behavior of fleeing from the tiger. In fact, there are so many ways for beliefs to be false (to fail to match up to reality), and only one way for beliefs to be true (to match up to the one reality that exists), that it would be surprising to discover that survival depends on true belief.

Plantinga calls naturalistic evolution a quasi-religion because it serves many of the roles of a religion, telling us about our origins and our ultimate nature. Plantinga's "naturalism defeated" argument purports to show that not all (quasi-)religions are created equal, epistemologically speaking. There are fountains that give you water, and then (as the prophet Jeremiah might put it) there are broken cisterns that don't give you water because they can hold no water. The prophet Isaiah regularly sued the wood, silver, and gold idols of the nations for false advertising—they claimed to see, hear, and predict the future, but were able to do no such thing, being blind, deaf, and mute. Plantinga is arguing that naturalistic evolution is a kind of *intellectual* idol that needs to be similarly exposed for not delivering on what it claims (knowledge and insight about our origins and nature) and therefore not being worthy of our trust.

7

PLANTINGA ON CHRISTIAN PHILOSOPHICAL METHOD

No Religious Neutrality

As we saw in chapter 1, Plantinga in his autobiographical "Self-Profile" (1985) repeatedly appeals enthusiastically to the notion that there is no such thing as religious neutrality when it comes to any sort of education or intellectual work. He agrees with the view of the Dutch Reformed churches in which he was raised "that education is essentially religious; there is such a thing as *secular* education but no such thing as an education that is both reasonably full-orbed and *religiously neutral*" (SP, 4). And, as we also saw, Plantinga was taught at Calvin College during his undergraduate days that

> the history of philosophy was at bottom an arena in which conflicting religious visions compete for human allegiance. Philosophy, as they saw it, was a matter of the greatest moment; for what it involved is both a struggle for men's souls and a fundamental expression of basic religious perspectives. (SP, 13)

(Plantinga repeats similar sentiments in his later intellectual autobiography, "A Christian Life Partly Lived" [CLPL], as well as in several interviews.)

Back in chapter 1, we noted that in his Notre Dame years in the early 1980s, Plantinga started to give deeper, more focused attention to the question of what it means to be a Christian philosopher, rather than being a philosopher who happens to be a Christian. Lurking in the background was the sense that if education cannot be religiously neutral, and if philosophy is ultimately a struggle among religious perspectives, then this must undoubtedly impact how a Christian goes about the philosophical task. But, as Plantinga also admits in his autobiographical writings, it is quite difficult to see at first glance what this amounts to. A Christian philosopher doesn't simply stand in the classroom and read the Bible out loud to the gathered students before commencing with Plato. Plantinga tells the delightful story of reading out a carefully crafted epistemology paper at a Tuesday colloquium at Calvin, only to have an earnest philosophy colleague turn to him and say, "You want to integrate Christianity and philosophy, right? Well, here's how you do it. After going through all these versions of the Verifiability Criterion [of meaning], you tell your class, 'So, as it says in Psalms 13, v. 1–3, "There is none that doeth good; no, not one"'" (SP, 31).

So how does one integrate Christianity and philosophy in a meaningful way? After giving this some thought, Plantinga summarized his method and aims as a Christian philosopher in a series of articles:

- 1984: "Advice to Christian Philosophers" (AdvCP)
- 1988: "Method in Christian Philosophy: A Reply" (MICP)
- 1992: "Augustinian Christian Philosophy" (AugCP)
- 1994: "On Christian Scholarship" (OCS)
- 1995: "Christian Philosophy at the End of the 20th Century" (CPE20C)

These present his vision for what a Christian philosopher is supposed to do and how to go about doing it.

Five Methodological Principles and Four Distinct Activities

The Principles

The first two articles give principles for the "how" of Christian philosophy, and the last three give content to the "what." Regarding the former, his general advice is that Christian philosophers should display more autonomy, integrity, and courage in the things they do and don't do as philosophers.[1] In particular,

- Christian philosophers *shouldn't*
    1. Restrict their intellectual projects to those pursued by unbelievers, or
    2. Take unbelieving assumptions as their starting assumptions, or
    3. Understand or reinterpret Christian belief so that it is palatable to unbelievers.
- Christian philosophers *should*
    4. Courageously pursue the questions, concerns, topics, agenda, and research programs of the Christian community, and even

1. One shouldn't misunderstand Plantinga's use of the term *autonomy*. In the philosophy of Cornelius Van Til, as he uses the term, autonomy is rightly seen as a bad thing, since we shouldn't be "a law unto ourselves" (*auto nomos*, or self-law), but instead submit to God's law. Plantinga is making the same point, but by commending autonomy he is commending independence from the world and its standards and commending submission to God. We should be autonomous or independent from the world in the intellectual standards we appeal to; Christian philosophers need to display more of that kind of independence. Plantinga does warn against autonomy, in roughly Van Til's sense of the term, in other contexts, speaking of "the age-old drive on the part of fallen humankind for autonomy and independence: autonomy and independence, among other things with respect to the demands of God" (OCS, 276).

5. Boldly start with Christian assumptions in their intellectual work (even if these aren't shared outside the Christian community).

Plantinga offers many specific illustrations of how these principles matter. Should a philosophy graduate student restrict her research into the nature of the mind by only seeking to develop currently popular materialist theories of the human person? No! Should she start by *assuming* that the way computers process input and produce output can provide her with a good model for the mind? No! To retain popularity should she *reinterpret* biblical passages about the soul and make them really about the body? No! Should she self-consciously seek a *Christian* understanding of the human person (one that, say, allows for life after death)? Yes! Should she start her investigations by assuming that there is life after death? Yes! As Plantinga points out, it takes independence, integrity, and courage to practice philosophy from this perspective, especially in a hostile environment, but honoring the Lord is at stake if we choose to ignore rather than implement these five principles. (In "Advice to Christian Philosophers," Plantinga applies these principles to how Christian philosophers should approach three topics in philosophy: the theory of meaning, the theory of knowledge, and the nature of human persons.)

The Activities

The last three articles give content to the "what" of Christian philosophy, continuously engaging in four different activities: Christian apologetics, philosophical theology, Christian philosophical criticism, and constructive, or positive, Christian philosophy.

Christian apologetics uses philosophy to *defend and support* Christian claims. (Some examples: to respond to the problem of evil, to give theistic arguments.) This is perhaps the broadest enterprise on the list and also the one most familiar to Christian nonphilosophers. Plantinga defines the activity of Christian apologetics both negatively ("defend Christianity against its detractors") and positively ("giving proof or arguments for the existence of God") (AugCP, 292–93). In the end, all Christian apologetics responds to people who allege a variation of the following assertion: "There are relevant intellectual norms, and Christianity doesn't satisfy them." How Christianity is alleged not to satisfy intellectual norms varies from critic to critic, of course:

- "Christianity is false." (That is, it's not true.)
- "Christianity is unjustified." (That is, we have no reason to think it's true.)
- "Christianity is incoherent." (That is, it just couldn't be true.)

Christian apologetics handles all these claims, with responses that seek to show not only that Christianity has nothing to fear from the realm of the intellect (or philosophy), but also that it can be supported by that realm. There are good arguments for the Christian faith, and no good arguments against it. A good slogan for Christian apologetics is therefore: "Theology supports and is not successfully challenged by philosophy."

Philosophical theology uses philosophy to *explain or illuminate* Christian claims. (Some examples: use philosophical distinctions, illustrations, or models to explain the Trinity, the incarnation, or the atonement.) Plantinga defines the activity of philosophical theology as "thinking about the central doctrines of the Christian faith from a philosophical perspective and employing the resources of philosophy" (AugCP, 291). Yes, God is three persons in one nature, but what does it take to be a "person" or a "nature"? Can we provide definitions of these terms that both summarize the relevant biblical material and shed light on something we want to understand about the Trinity? A good slogan for philosophical theology is therefore: "Philosophy illuminates theology."

Christian philosophical criticism uses philosophy to refute fundamental, worldview *alternatives* to Christian claims, while exposing the religious roots of such worldviews. (Some examples: refuting perennial naturalism, creative antirealism, and relativism—three non-Christian, indeed anti-Christian worldviews.) Plantinga notes that "vast stretches of contemporary philosophy . . . will have spiritual or religious roots—and spiritual and religious fruits," and since "these fruits may be unacceptable, or even noxious from the perspective of the Christian community," it follows that we need Christian philosophical criticism, defined as acting "to discern and understand these fruits, to test the spirits, to evaluate these philosophical constructions and contributions from a Christian point of view" (AugCP, 306). Good philosophy can be of help in this evaluation, exposing the inadequacies and religious nature of bad philosophy. A good slogan for Christian philosophical criticism is therefore: "Theology (with the help of good philosophy) exposes bad philosophy as bad theology."

Constructive, or *positive*, *Christian philosophy* answers philosophical questions *from the perspective of* Christian claims. (Some examples: develop theistic theories of otherwise philosophical topics: abstract objects, causality, natural laws, knowledge, mind, probability, subjunctive conditionals, science, freedom, human action, language, duty and human flourishing, love, beauty, play, and humor.) The common theme is that God's existence and activity make a difference to the distinctive philosophical account that Christians give of such things. Plantinga defines the activity of positive Christian philosophy as "thinking about and working out answers to the whole range of questions philosophers ask and answer . . . from an explicitly Christian point of view" (AugCP, 309). A good slogan for positive Christian philosophy is: "Theology encourages good philosophy."

We can also distinguish these activities by their result. Christian apologetics results in vindication of and support for theology. Philosophical theology results in a better understood theology. Christian philosophical criticism results in a negative evaluation of philosophical alternatives to Christianity. Positive Christian philosophy results in good philosophy from a Christian point of view.

Eight Ways to Approach the Truth of Distinctive Christian Claims

Introduction

The essentially religious nature of all substantive intellectual endeavor, when applied to philosophy, leads Plantinga to endorse five methodological principles that guide Christian philosophers in four distinct activities. The central idea here is that one's religion and philosophy need to be *integrated* with each other, not practiced in isolation from each other. To do the latter is impossible, and to even attempt it is impious.

But what does the truth of Christianity have to do with pursuing these activities according to these principles? In particular, how does the fifth principle, of starting with Christian claims, get used within the fourfold activity of Christian philosophy? Perhaps surprisingly, this is not an easy question to answer, and having now surveyed Plantinga's philosophical work in the previous five chapters, the results seem to be mixed. While a lot of Plantinga's writing is *about* the truth of distinctive Christian claims in one way or another, very little of it relies on actually *asserting* the truth of Christian claims. Is this a problem?

To begin answering this important question, consider eight different ways in which the truth of distinctive Christian claims can relate to the task of the Christian philosopher. In the list below, these are correlated with the four activities of Christian philosophy (with the broad activity of Christian apologetics being covered by the first five ways):

- Christian apologetics (the defense of the faith): ways 1–5
- Philosophical theology (philosophy illuminating theology): way 6
- Christian philosophical criticism (theology critiquing bad philosophy): way 7
- Constructive Christian philosophy (theology encouraging good philosophy): way 8

The Eight Ways

1. *Christian apologetics as transcendent truth*: The truth of distinctive Christian claims is assumed as premises in the arguments typically forwarded (1) in support of Christianity, (2) in defense of Christianity against rival views, or (3) against the rival views themselves.
    - Possible examples include:
        - Cornelius Van Til's use of "transcendental" arguments for Christian theism
        - Carl F. Henry's appeal to the "axioms of revelation" against non-Christian views
        - Gordon Clark's "scripturalism"—deriving all knowledge claims from the Scriptures alone
    - No examples from Plantinga

2. *Christian apologetics as proof*: The truth of distinctive Christian claims can be directly inferred (either deductively or inductively) from many other things we typically accept. But the truth of these Christian claims is not appealed to as premises in these arguments.

- Examples include:
  - Thomas Aquinas's deductive natural theology
  - Richard Swinburne's inductive natural theology
  - Many similar works from other authors
- No examples from Plantinga

3. *Christian apologetics as support*: The truth of distinctive Christian claims can be supported (though perhaps not inferred) from many other things we typically accept. But the truth of these Christian claims is not appealed to as premises in these arguments.
   - Examples from Plantinga:
     - Direct support: "Two Dozen (or so) Theistic Arguments"
     - Direct support: fine-tuning, design discourse (*Where the Conflict Really Lies,* chs. 7–8)
     - Indirect support: theism accounting for the fundamental assumptions of natural science (*Where the Conflict Really Lies,* ch. 9)

4. *Christian apologetics as rational acceptability*: The truth of distinctive Christian claims can be shown to be rationally acceptable by philosophical argumentation (though perhaps not shown to be likely to be true, or even evidentially supported). But the truth of these Christian claims is not appealed to as premises in these arguments.
   - Examples from Plantinga:
     - Parity argument from God and other minds
     - Modal ontological argument for God's existence

5. *Christian apologetics as coherence*: Distinctive Christian claims can be shown by argument to be consistent with each other and with other important things we typically

accept. But the truth of these Christian claims is not appealed to as premises in these arguments.

- Examples include:
    - Swinburne's *The Coherence of Theism*
    - Many similar works from other authors
- Examples from Plantinga:
    - Reformulation of divine simplicity to avoid incoherence
    - Defense of the logical compatibility of God and evil in the free will defense
    - Defense of properly basic belief in God against the evidentialist objection
    - Defense of divine omniscience from the free will / foreknowledge dilemma
    - Defense of divine omniscience from Cantorian paradoxes
    - Defense of the possible warrant of Christian belief against objections from Freud, Marx, postmodernism, and pluralism, in *Warranted Christian Belief*
    - Defense of the rationality of belief in God against the evidential problem of evil, by critiquing the theories of probability used in the latter and by skeptical theism
    - "Reducing the perplexity surrounding human suffering and evil" by using supralapsarian, "O felix culpa" theodicy
    - Refutation of alleged and superficial conflict between divine creation, divine action (both providential and miraculous), and scriptural inspiration (on the one hand), and biology, physics, evolutionary psychology, and historical Bible criticism (on the other hand), in chapters 1–6 of *Where the Conflict Really Lies*

6. *Philosophical theology*: The content of distinctive Christian claims can be further explained and clarified by the resources of philosophy. But the truth of these Christian claims is not appealed to as premises in these arguments.
   - Examples include:
     - Augustine on the Trinity
     - Anselm on the incarnation
     - Aquinas on divine simplicity
     - The developed philosophical-theological models of the Trinity, incarnation, atonement, providence, inspiration of Scripture, resurrection, anthropological dualism, petitionary prayer, etc., which have been developed by many others during the past forty years
   - Examples from Plantinga:
     - Use of foundationalism to develop a model of natural knowledge of God
     - Use of proper function epistemology to develop a model of Christian conversion
     - Use of possible worlds metaphysics to develop a model of God's greatness

7. *Christian philosophical criticism*: The truth of distinctive Christian claims is not challenged by alternatives to those claims, because we can refute them. But the truth of these Christian claims is not appealed to as premises in these arguments.
   - Examples include:
     - C. S. Lewis's argument against pantheism
     - William L. Craig's argument against the eternity of the world
     - J. P. Moreland's arguments against naturalist theories of consciousness

    - Swinburne's argument against physicalist theories of mind
    - Robin Collins's arguments against the multiverse hypothesis
- Examples from Plantinga:
    - Argument against naturalistic evolution as epistemologically self-defeating, in chapter 10 of *Where the Conflict Really Lies*
    - Argument against theological agnosticism as conceptually incoherent, in chapters 1–2 of *Warranted Christian Belief*
    - Argument against materialist understanding of human beings as metaphysically impossible

8. *Positive Christian philosophy*: The truth of distinctive Christian claims is *assumed for the sake of argument*, in order to explore what other claims—about the world and within various intellectual disciplines—might look like if these Christian claims were true. But the truth of these Christian claims is not appealed to as premises in these arguments.
    - Examples from Plantinga:
        - Philosophically modeling how Christian belief can get its warrant, by drawing upon theology (the *sensus divinitatis* and the internal instigation of the Holy Spirit)
        - Philosophically modeling (most) ordinary causation in the world, by drawing upon theology (divine occasionalism)
        - Philosophically modeling the ontology of sets, by drawing upon theology (a divine activity of "collecting together")
        - Philosophically modeling the laws of nature, by drawing upon theology (the necessity of God's

power and the contingency of God's will in creation)

- Philosophically modeling the efficacy and accessibility of mathematics, by drawing upon theology (God's creating man in the *imago dei*)

Does Plantinga's Own Christian Philosophy Exemplify His Method?

A number of things can be clearly seen from the list above.

First, Plantinga's work exemplifies ways 3–8 of connecting the truth of distinctive Christian claims with philosophical practice. Examples can be given for each. But it is hard to find an argument in Plantinga that draws upon the truth of Christianity as a premise (way 1). It is also hard to find an argument in Plantinga in which he claims to show, either deductively or inductively, that distinctive Christian claims are true (way 2). As we saw in chapter 4, he rejects the idea of deduction as the standard of success for theistic arguments, and what he thinks about "the principle of dwindling probabilities" seems to indicate that he would be unimpressed by many inductive attempts to prove God's existence as well.[2]

Second, Plantinga has robustly engaged in all four activities that he sees as composing Christian philosophy, despite not engaging in ways 1 or 2. He pursues Christian apologetics in ways 3–5, philosophical theology in way 6, Christian philosophical criticism

2. Advocates of way (1) would be disappointed to learn that Plantinga doesn't really "start with" Christian claims in the way they do. But it would take additional argument to show that Plantinga's contributions to Christian apologetics in ways 3–5 are inconsistent with a way 1 approach. Perhaps these different ways are simply doing different things. A lecture about the incarnation is not a lecture about the Trinity. But a lecture about the incarnation is not thereby incompatible with a lecture about the Trinity, simply because it fails to mention the Trinity. Likewise, a proof that Christian claims are rational is not a transcendental proof from Christian claims to the impossibility of the contrary. But the failure of the former to be the latter doesn't seem to be a refutation of the former! The different approaches are doing different things.

in way 7, and constructive Christian philosophy in way 8. We can compile an impressively full list of ways in which Plantinga has pursued the entire range of Christian philosophy as he defines it, even if he has not practiced every way of doing so.

Third, Plantinga's work exemplifies all the methodological principles that he has advised other Christian philosophers to follow, with the apparent exception of the fifth principle. He has followed his own advice in not restricting his projects to those pursued by unbelievers, or taking unbelieving assumptions as his starting point, or reinterpreting Christian belief so that it is palatable to unbelievers. And, positively, he has pursued questions and topics of central concern to the Christian community.

But with respect to his fifth (last) principle, *does* he start with Christian assumptions in his intellectual work? That depends on what we mean by "start with." If we mean "assert the truth of the claims as premises in arguments for the claims" (for example, appeal to the truth that God exists in order to prove by argument that God exists), then, as we saw in our eight-point list above, he does not do that. (Plantinga would probably say that this would beg the question, that is, assume what is to be proved.) But does he start with the truth of Christian claims in a broader sense? Here are four ways to answer yes:

- Does he think that it is entirely natural and appropriate for Christians to accept God's existence and the truth of the Bible without first proving to themselves by argument that such claims are true? Yes.
- Does he think that the truth of Christian truth claims constrains the kind of philosophical explanations and accounts that we should accept for ourselves or offer to others? Yes.
- Does he think that Christians, in coming to find out what position is best supported by the evidence, should be free to draw upon all that they know from the Bible? Yes.

- Is he strongly motivated by his firm prior acceptance of Christian truth claims to engage in Christian apologetics—supporting Christian truth claims by argument and defending them from criticism? Yes.

Fourth, even granting this broader understanding of "start with," is it really the case that Plantinga's philosophy focuses mainly upon, and relates to the truth of, distinctive Christian claims? To be sure, Plantinga *says* that focusing on distinctive Christian claims is essential to his method. In "Advice to Christian Philosophers," he is exceptionally clear that what matters are "the fundamental truths of Christianity," or "Christian doctrine," or "a Christian perspective," "Christian thought," "Christian ways of thinking," and "a *Christian* and *theistic* point of view" (AdvCP, 264–70). Likewise, in "Method in Christian Philosophy: A Reply," he repeatedly focuses on "an explicitly Christian or theistic perspective," "a Christian or theistic way of looking at the world," "Christian beliefs," "Christian doctrine," "beliefs as a Christian," "one's Christian beliefs," "the beliefs one holds as a Christian," "Christian supernaturalism," "a Christian view of God and man and the world," "specifically Christian topics," "an explicitly Christian and theistic perspective," "the Christian faith as we understand it," "the Christian understanding of God," and "traditional Christianity" (MICP, 159–64). Similar references to Christian things occur throughout all the other sources for Plantinga's philosophical method noted at the beginning of this chapter.

But now look at the examples from Plantinga listed under the eight numbered ways above (or considered in previous chapters). Virtually *all* of these examples are about defending, arguing, or explaining either the truth of theism, or the coherence of theism, or alternatives to theism, or the coherence of a generic theistic attribute, or basic belief in theism, or reconciling theistic belief with science. There are, in fact, just two exceptions to this generalization: Plantinga's "extended Aquinas/Calvin model" of how belief in "the great things of the gospel" by way of the Holy Spirit's work can be a warranted belief (see ways 5 and 8), and his appeal to the unsurpassed value of any world with incarnation and atonement as a way of reducing the intellectual perplexity generated by the evil in the world (see way 5). But apart from these two exceptions, the entirety of Plantinga's philosophical work points away from specific Christian belief and is instead directed to theism.

There are at least two ways to respond to this discovery. Uncharitably, we might conclude that Plantinga's obsession with specifically Christian beliefs when explaining his methodology is just for show. Perhaps all he really cares about is defending and developing theistic belief, but he advertises his philosophical work as specifically Christian because doing so will generate more support and sympathy among Christian students, colleagues, and churches. (Perhaps we can throw in a pious, sincere, but misguided attempt to bolster the faith and self-confidence of Christians, specifically.) Or, alternatively, and more charitably, we can discern something else: using philosophy to defend, support, illuminate, and make application of specifically Christian belief is *an extremely hard task*. There are mysteries and then there are mysteries, and perhaps the Christian doctrines of Trinity, incarnation, and atonement are closer to the latter. One has one's hands full just arguing about God. This wouldn't be to say that no one has implemented Plantinga's vision for specifically Christian philosophy. There is currently a flourishing philosophical literature offering accounts, defenses, and application of the three doctrines just named, and many more besides, and many of the participants in those discussions wouldn't have joined up if it hadn't been for the bold stance of Plantinga and others in recent decades. It's just to say that Plantinga himself hasn't offered up philosophical accounts of Trinity, incarnation, and atonement.

Still, there are those two specifically Christian contributions I listed earlier, and those contributions are enormous. (One of them is literally five hundred pages long!) Each has generated a large amount of fruitful and worthwhile discussion that continues today. Relating the incarnation and the atonement to the question of God's relation to the evil in the world, and offering an account of how we come to believe in the great things of the gospel (and are warranted in doing so), are philosophical contributions with specific Christian content. And each utilizes insights from past generations of specifically Christian thinkers. Rather than hang his head in shame that he hasn't philosophized about every Christian doctrine, Plantinga would no doubt urge others to enter into this challenging work to which he and others have contributed.

8

PLANTINGA AND THE REFORMED HERITAGE

Each of the books in the Great Thinkers series aims to provide critical analysis of the thinker from a Reformed Christian perspective. This isn't because the Reformed locate infallibility in their own tradition. To adapt something I've said elsewhere about another Christian philosopher:

> Only the Scriptures are inspired and ultimately authoritative; every other source of insight is hit-and-miss. Working out a consistent approach in Christian apologetics might lead you to be *selective* in following any noncanonical thinker of the past. In doing so, these uninspired-but-useful thinkers find their proper place—neither above you nor below you but by your side.[1]

1. Greg Welty, "Richard Swinburne: Pioneering Analytic Apologetics," in *The History of Apologetics: A Biographical and Methodological Introduction*, ed. Benjamin K. Forrest, Joshua D. Chatraw, and Alister E. McGrath (Grand Rapids: Zondervan Academic, 2020), 726.

But while both Plantinga and the Reformed tradition are fallible, that is quite compatible with being eminently useful. Indeed, evaluating Plantinga from a Reformed perspective makes sense not only in the context of this book series, but also given this particular thinker. As we saw in chapter 1, Plantinga had a Dutch Reformed upbringing, weekly catechism classes, and college education, and later returned to Calvin College to teach philosophy for twenty years in that Dutch Reformed context. By his own confession, the Reformed tradition exerted a strong influence over his intellectual outlook and methodology. It is of intrinsic interest to locate Plantinga within that tradition, noting any contributions to it or departures from it.

This chapter identifies five Reformed themes and asks two questions about each one. First, to what extent does Plantinga's work support this theme? Second, if Plantinga's work is in tension with this theme, how easily can his arguments be supplemented or revised to remove this tension? Quite understandably, different readers may draw the lines differently from me, particularly when considering my later distinctions between Reformed themes and Reformed essentials. But in the end, having surveyed Plantinga's philosophical work, I sense that significant debate over Plantinga's relation to the Reformed tradition will likely be about these five themes, and I hope this chapter provides a succinct overview that would be useful for any future discussion on the topic.

Human Freedom

Plantinga's Appeal to Libertarian Free Will

Assuming that we are morally responsible and have the kind of free will needed for such responsibility, Christians divide into two camps: those who say our free will is incompatible with determinism, and those who say it is compatible with determinism. The former endorse "libertarian free will" (LFW), whereas the latter endorse "compatibilist free will" (CFW). It is a commonplace that the Reformed tradition emphatically rejects LFW and embraces CFW instead. But Plantinga is firmly in the LFW camp, which seems to place him at odds with the Reformed tradition. Indeed, when discussing differences between Plantinga and the Reformed tradition, this is usually the first thing to be brought up!

It seems obvious that Plantinga *is* outside the Reformed tradition on this point, as it is hard to reconcile the existence of creaturely LFW with the pervasive, meticulous, divine foreordination of all things (taught in the Westminster Confession of Faith, chapter 3, "Of God's Eternal Decree"), or with the responsibility of sinners to believe the gospel despite being totally unable to do so (taught in the Canons of Dordt, Third and Fourth Main Points of Doctrine, articles 3 and 9). If, as libertarians say, we are the ultimate cause of our choices, and we could have chosen otherwise in the same exact circumstances, then there seems no place for a divine decree in which God (and not creatures) ultimately determines whatsoever comes to pass.[2]

In his philosophical writings, Plantinga puts LFW to work mainly in addressing the problem of evil. We saw in chapter 3 that his most celebrated and influential response to the logical problem of evil is the "free will defense" (FWD), according to which (1) it's possible that there are truths about how we would use our freedom in various circumstances, and (2) it's possible that such truths reveal the following to be the case:

2. For a powerful argument that LFW is contrary to the Reformed confessional tradition, see James N. Anderson and Paul Manata, "Determined to Come Most Freely: Some Challenges for Libertarian Calvinism," *Journal of Reformed Theology* 11, no. 3 (2017): 272–97. Could Molinism do the trick? Perhaps, but that is excluded by the Reformed tradition as well (see the second Reformed theme below).

> *r*: For any free creature available to God to create, that creature is such that if it were to be created it would do at least one morally bad thing.

Plantinga uses the possibility of *r* to prove that God and evil are logically consistent, contrary to what atheists like J. L. Mackie have claimed. And Plantinga is clear that the sense of "free" in claims like *r* is libertarian freedom:

> If a person is free with respect to a given action, then he is free to perform that action and free to refrain from performing it; no antecedent conditions and/or causal laws determine that he will perform the action, or that he won't. It is within his power, at the time in question, to take or perform the action and within his power to refrain from it. (*GFE*, 29)

What If There Is No Libertarian Free Will?

It is widely assumed that Plantinga's strategy in the FWD involves his appealing to the existence of LFW, but a closer look reveals that he is only appealing to its *possible* existence. Plantinga's FWD is a *defense* (giving God's possible reason for permitting evil), not a *theodicy* (giving God's actual reason for permitting evil). To make the FWD work, all one needs is the *possibility* of LFW, not its actuality. As Plantinga himself notes, "In arguing that the existence of a wholly good, omniscient and omnipotent God is compatible with evil *simpliciter*, I am not committed to our actually having libertarian freedom, although, of course, I do believe that we do" (AWalls, 623).

Still, even if Plantinga's FWD doesn't assume the existence of LFW, it does assume that it is possible for LFW to exist. What does the Reformed tradition say about that? On the one hand, maybe this kind of freedom is intrinsically unintelligible and therefore impossible, because it requires finite creatures to perform an infinite regress of acts of will. (This seems to be part of Jonathan Edwards's argument against Arminians in *The Freedom of the Will.*) But, on the other hand, perhaps as long as God has LFW—grace wouldn't be grace, if God couldn't refrain from giving it—then it is a possible kind of freedom, even if humans don't actually have it. And again, the FWD only needs the possibility of LFW.

Plantinga's FWD also assumes that LFW has extraordinary *value*: "A world containing creatures who are significantly free (and freely perform more good than evil actions) is more valuable, all else being equal, than a world containing no free creatures at all" (*GFE*, 30). Here, Reformed Christians might push back: if LFW is so valuable, why didn't God create the world with it? Given all this, let's assume for the sake of argument that for the Reformed, LFW is nonexistent, impossible, and lacks value. How would that affect Plantinga's philosophical contributions? Well, we would lose Plantinga's FWD. And since one of his five replies to the evidential problem of evil adapts the FWD, we would lose that too. But that's all that is lost, as far as I can tell. Plenty still remains: his first undercutting defeater for the logical problem of evil, and his four other replies to the evidential argument. LFW is just not as central to Plantinga's arguments as many seem to think.[3]

Divine Providence

Supralapsarianism

We saw in chapter 3 that one of Plantinga's replies to the evidential problem of evil is to endorse a supralapsarian theodicy, according to which God's decree to provide salvation is logically prior to (and therefore explanatory of) his decrees to create and to permit the fall. God first and foremost aimed at salvation realities

3. See chapter 3 for the details on these five replies that would remain. Also see T. Ryan Byerly, "Free Will Theodicies for Theological Determinists," *Sophia* 56, no. 2 (2017): 289–310.

(like incarnation and atonement), because of their relevance in bringing about an extraordinarily valuable world. Because this overarching divine purpose requires there to be a fall into sin, Plantinga can explain why God permits evil: it is because God's goodness aims at bringing about the most valuable kind of world possible.

Plantinga's sudden embrace of supralapsarianism nearly fifty years into his writing career took many of his contemporaries by surprise, particularly given his advocacy of LFW (see above). But there is no doubt that his argument here draws upon—as he puts it—one of "the tenets of a certain sort of Calvinism" (SOFC, 363). Yet two things should be noted. First, while it is primarily the Reformed community which debates this particular issue, presumably there is a place for infralapsarianism in that community as well. So, taking the position Plantinga does (supralapsarianism rather than infralapsarianism) is not a Reformed essential. Second, while supralapsarianism has been most highly developed within the Reformed tradition, the roots of this perspective seem to transcend the Reformed community, for what that's worth, since the Latin title for the theodicy ("O felix culpa") comes from the liturgy for the Roman Catholic Easter Vigil.

Molinism

There are not only providential schemes that the Reformed tradition includes (supralapsarianism and infralapsarianism), but also schemes that it excludes—and Molinism seems to be one of them. Named after the sixteenth-century Jesuit priest Luis de Molina, Molinism says that God consults his "middle knowledge" when formulating his decree for how the universe will turn out. Such middle knowledge tells God what (libertarian) free creatures would choose in various circumstances. Knowing this, God then creates and places free creatures in just those situations in which he knows how they would use their freedom. Middle knowledge enables God to meticulously plan a universe that has creaturely LFW in it.

Molinism seems flatly incompatible with the Reformed tradition. According to the Westminster Confession of Faith, 3.2, God surely has conditional knowledge: "God knows whatsoever may or can come to pass upon all supposed conditions." But God's decree isn't based on conditional knowledge: he has "not decreed anything because he foresaw it as . . . that which would come to pass upon such conditions." Likewise, according to the Canons of Dordt, First Main Point of Doctrine, articles 9 and 10, God's decree of election isn't "based on a prerequisite cause or condition in the person to be chosen," such as the condition that the person would exercise faith in various circumstances.

What does any of this have to do with Plantinga? Well, his FWD appeals to at least the *possibility* that God governs his universe in a Molinist manner. According to the FWD, it's possible that God's middle knowledge reveals that something like *r* is the case, and so if he wants a world with moral good in it, he's stuck with moral evil as well, and he plans the universe accordingly. But as with LFW, so here: Plantinga is only arguing for a *possibility*. Can't we be Calvinist in our convictions, but Molinist in our imaginings? What's so bad about that? Plantinga isn't endorsing this scheme of providence as true, but raising it as a possibility that the atheist has overlooked. Can the atheist exclude the possibility of such truths?

Still, the mere possibility of middle knowledge would rightly make many in the Reformed tradition uncomfortable, for two reasons. First, such truths just don't seem possible. Even if there could be LFW, how could there be a truth, like *r*, about how we would specifically use it? What would make a claim like *r* true? God's nature doesn't make *r* true, because God's nature is necessary and *r* is contingent (being about free will, it could be otherwise). God's will doesn't make *r* true, because then he could just will that no LFW gets used badly, and the problem of evil remains. Existing people can't make *r* true, since presumably God consults *r* to figure out whether to make people in the first place! We've run out of truthmakers. It seems as if Plantinga must insist that nothing would make claims like *r* true; rather, possibly it just *is* true, and that is that. But that is a very odd thing to claim. It would be like saying that Alvin Plantinga makes the following claim true: <In circumstances C, Plantinga freely does X>, but that nothing makes the following (very similar) claim true: <If Plantinga were in circumstances C, Plantinga would freely do X>. And that seems crazy, since both of these claims are equally specific, equally about Plantinga, equally contingent, and equally about the same free will choice. Why would the first need a truthmaker (Plantinga's actual choice), but the second would not? In the end, Molinism would require us to say that *r* can be true for no reason at all, and that just doesn't seem reasonable.

Second, such truths seem flatly incompatible with God's omnipotence. Claim *r* implies that God is unable to actualize multitudes of possible worlds (any world where no creature uses LFW for evil). Should we agree that it's even possible that God fails to have the power to actualize these worlds (that is, that *r* could be true)? Plantinga takes a different view here. Since the freedom being talked about is libertarian, God can't directly cause anybody to use it in a certain way. By definition, no one other than the agent can cause his acts of LFW. But if there are truths like AP: <If Plantinga were in circumstances C, Plantinga would freely do X>, then their truth would enhance God's creative and providential opportunities, according to Plantinga. God could now indirectly bring about Plantinga's specific free will choice, by creating him and putting him in C. So rather than diminishing God's power, Plantinga would claim that truths like AP would enhance the range of God's power. Still, something doesn't seem right here. If *r* were true, wouldn't God be extremely unlucky? If so, doesn't Molinism say that God is subject to a massive amount of luck? Is that appropriate for a supremely perfect being who is worthy of worship?

Since these problems might give anyone reason to think that Molinism isn't even possible, they offer the Reformed a second reason to reject Plantinga's FWD (beyond his use of LFW). Of course, as before, loss of the FWD still leaves at least five of Plantinga's seven replies to the problem of evil intact, and that is no small thing. In addition, there are worse providential schemes to adopt. Molinism brings the libertarian much closer to Calvinist providence than just about any other libertarian Christian view (since it is comprehensively decretal), and that is no small thing either!

Implicitly, Plantinga appeals to Molinism in one other context. We saw in chapter 5 that Plantinga's Ockhamist solution to the free will / foreknowledge dilemma seemed to depend on the cogency of a Molinist perspective on providence: "It is possible that if God had foreseen that you would choose *that* alternative, he would have acted very differently. Perhaps he would have created different persons; perhaps, indeed, he would not have created Abraham" (OWO, 257). If Plantinga's Ockhamism requires Molinism, that gives the Reformed reason to give up that argument as well. But, of course, the Reformed have no need of a solution to the free will / foreknowledge dilemma, Ockhamist or otherwise, because that dilemma assumes we have LFW. The Reformed would say there is no dilemma if our freedom is compatibilist!

Regeneration Precedes Faith

The Extended A/C Model of Christian Faith

As we saw in chapter 2, just as Plantinga argued in 1983 that belief in God could be "properly basic," so in 2000 he argued the same for the full panoply of distinctive Christian belief. His "extended A/C [Aquinas/Calvin] model" says that belief in "the great things of the gospel" (Trinity, incarnation, atonement, justification) is produced by the "internal instigation of the Holy Spirit." This is not only how Christian faith *normally* arises, but how it *must* arise, because in a fallen world nothing other than the power of the Holy Spirit can overcome the cognitive, affective, and volitional effects of sin upon our minds and hearts, and therefore overcome our robust commitment to suppress the truth in unrighteousness.

After initially presenting his model, Plantinga spends three chapters in *Warranted Christian Belief* explaining the "cognitive consequences of sin" and our need for "cognitive renewal" and the "renewal and redirection" of our affections by the Holy Spirit. To make his case, Plantinga draws upon deeply Reformed insights about God the Holy Spirit as the cause of faith. While Scripture is cited first and foremost, he also draws upon Calvin's *Institutes,* Henry Scougal's *The Life of God in the Soul of Man,* Jonathan Edwards's *Religious Affections,* and Abraham Kuyper's *To Be Near unto God.* (He also cites Augustine, Aquinas, Luther, Wesley, C. S. Lewis, and John Piper.)

It certainly looks as if Plantinga is enthusiastically agreeing with, and then applying in an epistemological context, the classic Reformed doctrine that regeneration precedes faith. Surely much of that doctrine is there, and it is rare to find an influential Christian philosopher making so much Reformed truth central to his epistemology. However, that doctrine is widely understood as including the view that the Holy Spirit's work in Christian conversion is not only necessary for the production of faith, but sufficient for it. We have "wholly lost *all* ability of will to *any* spiritual good accompanying salvation," an unbeliever cannot even "prepare himself" for conversion, and man is "*altogether* passive therein, until, being quickened and renewed by the Holy Spirit, he is thereby enabled to answer this call" (Westminster Confession of Faith, 9.3 and 10.1–2, emphasis added).

Is a Free Act of Will Necessary for Faith?

In an excellent discussion of whether, in Plantinga, "faith depends on a free choice of the will," Dewey Hoitenga argues,

"Plantinga sprinkles his otherwise determinist discussion with language that suggests that a free act of the will is also a necessary condition for the 'production' of faith."[4] What this means is that

> though the language of Plantinga's theory of warranted revealed belief is significantly determinist, it is not consistently so. In developing his theory of warrant for revealed beliefs, he invokes side by side . . . two conflicting theories of the will: a determinist theory, on which God *alone causes* the formation of faith by a regeneration of the noetic faculties (intellect and will); but also something of a free will theory, on which God *offers* the gift of salvation, and even *enables* the noetic faculties to believe, but stops short of causing the formation of that faith.[5]

Two quotations from Plantinga seem to bear out this assessment. First: "Like the regeneration of which it is a part, faith is a gift; it is given to anyone *who is willing to accept it*" (*WCB*, 244, emphasis added). Second:

> Under what circumstances would the Holy Spirit have *failed*, with respect to a given person, to do this work of enabling one to see the truth of the great things of the gospel? The model need take no stand on this issue, but it is part of much traditional Christian teaching to hold that a necessary condition of my receiving the gift of faith is my acquiescing, being willing to accept the gift, being prepared to receive it. There is a contribution to this process that I myself must make, a contribution that I can withhold. (*WCB*, 257)

4. Dewey Hoitenga, "Christian Theism: Ultimate Reality and Meaning in the Philosophy of Alvin Plantinga," *Ultimate Reality and Meaning* 23, no. 3 (September 2000): 228–29.

5. Hoitenga, "Christian Theism," 230.

This element of Plantinga's extended A/C model, which makes the gift of faith dependent on my independent contribution to the conversion process, seems in considerable tension with the Reformed doctrine of the effectual call. How should the Reformed community receive this feature of his views? First, it should be stressed that this is the *only* element of the model that seems in tension with the Reformed tradition. Throughout his presentation, Plantinga uses causal language *par excellence* to describe the Holy Spirit's work in illuminating our minds, regenerating our hearts, and producing faith in us. It shouldn't be overlooked that this is a fundamentally Reformed view, and arguably the centerpiece of his most important contribution to Christian epistemology. Second, it is trivially easy to just *add* to Plantinga's model the view that the Holy Spirit's work is not only necessary but sufficient for faith. Indeed, Plantinga himself indicates this possibility in the second quote above, since "the model need take no stand on this issue." Since Plantinga's model can be easily adapted to include this claim, the cogency of the model and of the overall argument it serves isn't affected by this controversy. It can easily be made compatible with the Reformed tradition.

Reformed Apologetics

Rejecting Neutrality

Four ideas arguably compose a distinctively Reformed vision for Christian apologetics: no neutrality in intellectual endeavor, the *sensus divinitatis* in all men, the rejection of classical natural theology, and the embrace of transcendental arguments for God. To take these ideas in order, consider first the matter of neutrality. As we saw in Plantinga's reflections on his own upbringing (chapter 1) and on the method and activity of Christian philosophy as he conceives it (chapter 7), he strongly believes that there is no such thing as "religious neutrality" in education or intellectual work. He traces this view to the Dutch Reformed traditions in which he was raised. Philosophy is "a struggle for men's souls and a fundamental expression of basic religious perspectives" (SP, 13). This commitment is seen in Plantinga's work in three main ways.

First, the thesis of no neutrality generates his five methodological principles, or the "how" of Christian philosophy: don't (1) restrict projects to what unbelievers pursue, (2) start with unbelieving assumptions, or (3) interpret Christian belief to satisfy unbelievers; do (4) pursue the Christian community's questions and topics, and (5) start with Christian assumptions.

Second, the no neutrality thesis also helps define for Plantinga the fourfold activity of philosophy, or the "what" of Christian philosophy. This is not so clear with the first two activities. Neither Christian apologetics (theology supported and not successfully challenged by philosophy) nor philosophical theology (philosophy illuminating theology) has to start with Christian assumptions, on Plantinga's view. Rather, in these activities it seems to be philosophy (and related knowledge disciplines, such as science) that supports, defends, and illuminates theology. But no neutrality does seem to characterize the last two activities. Christian philosophical criticism (exposing bad philosophy as bad theology) is aimed at exposing the *religious* roots of non-Christian worldviews, while positive Christian philosophy (theology encouraging good philosophy) develops explicitly *theological* perspectives on central philosophical questions.[6]

Third, and descending now to specifics, Plantinga's arguments and conclusions often illustrate the no neutrality thesis. According to chapter 2 (on faith and reason), allegedly neutral criteria of rationality typically hide an anti-religious bias, arguments against the warrant of Christian belief presuppose the falsity of Christian

6. The reader is encouraged to review the discussion of these five principles and four activities in chapter 7.

belief, and epistemological disputes may ultimately be metaphysical or theological disputes. According to chapter 4 (on theistic arguments), theology can inform the best theories of laws of nature, mathematics, and causation.[7] According to chapter 6 (on religion and science), arguments for conflict between science and religion involve unbelievers adding quasi-religious assumptions to scientific theories, and the natural sciences presuppose many theological assumptions. Plantinga doesn't just *claim* unbelievers aren't neutral. He *shows* it, perhaps more so than many Christian philosophers contemporaneous with him.

In conclusion, Plantinga's work strongly supports this Reformed theme, with the possible caveat that the no neutrality thesis is not as clearly aligned with Christian apologetics or philosophical theology as it is with the other activities of Christian philosophy, as Plantinga conceives it.

The *Sensus Divinitatis*

As we saw in chapter 2, Plantinga thinks that faith is just as much a form of knowledge as reason, and he seeks to demonstrate this by drawing upon Calvin's doctrine of the *sensus divinitatis* (sense of the divine) in the *Institutes*, 1.3.1. His argument exploits an obvious analogy between the *sensus divinitatis* and empirical perception, in that there is no noncircular argument for the reliability of either faculty. Rather, theistic and perceptual beliefs are both properly basic and perfectly acceptable to hold apart from argument.

Perhaps sensing the obvious truth that Calvin is within the Reformed tradition if anyone is, Plantinga initially labeled these views as a "Reformed epistemology" held by "Reformed epistemologists." He used these terms twenty-six times in published papers

7. The topic of causation wasn't touched on in chapter 4 or elsewhere in this book, but finds separate treatment in Plantinga's 2016 paper, "Law, Cause, and Occasionalism" (LCO).

between 1980 and 1983, along with "Calvinist epistemology" (SP, 55, 93). But faced with evidence that even Thomas Aquinas endorsed a kind of immediate or intuitive knowledge of God that can be had apart from argument, Plantinga later came to believe that his early labeling was a misnomer:

> I wish to remark parenthetically that I regret having referred to this project, half in jest, as "Reformed Epistemology" or "Calvinist Epistemology"; some didn't realize this was supposed to be just a clever title, not a gauntlet thrown at the feet of Catholic philosophers. (CLPL, 67)

And:

> I'm inclined to regret the choice of the name: some have apparently thought the idea was to cast a gauntlet at the feet of Roman Catholic philosophers. Nothing could be further from the truth. As a matter of fact I think Calvin and Thomas Aquinas are very close on matters epistemological, in particular on matters concerning the epistemology of Christian belief. In [my forthcoming] *Warranted Christian Belief* I propose a model under which specifically Christian belief can have warrant, and (to note that concord) call it the "Aquinas-Calvin model." (AW, 354 fn. 4)

Of course, Plantinga's earliest work on the topic had already indicated this. Speaking about our immediate, noninferential knowledge of God, Plantinga said, "Perhaps here we must see Aquinas as an early Calvinist" (RBG, 47), since Aquinas speaks of such knowledge in *Summa contra gentiles* 3.38. Or again:

> I say "Reformed thinkers"; in fact, however, there is a tradition in Christian thought going all the way back to Bonaventura,

> Anselm and Augustine according to which belief in God doesn't need the evidential support of other sources of belief; it is in order just as it stands. (SP, 96 fn. 27)

Nevertheless, no matter what the label, Plantinga's "Reformed epistemology" incorporates a distinctively Reformed theme (if Calvin counts for anything). What seems to be a misnomer is that it is an epistemology, or a full-blown theory of knowledge. It's not. Rather, it's a (deservedly much discussed) argument on a fairly narrow topic: the evidentialist objection to the rationality of theistic belief overlooks the possibility that belief in God may be properly basic because it is produced by the *sensus divinitatis*. That's it. For Plantinga's epistemology proper we have to look to the three *Warrant* volumes published in 1993 and 2000.

Rejecting Classical Natural Theology

As we saw in chapter 4, early in his career Plantinga vigorously and negatively evaluated the three main traditional arguments for God (Aquinas's cosmological argument, Anselm's ontological argument, and the teleological argument discussed by Hume) (*GOM*, chs. 1–4). He has never endorsed the classical project of proofs of God's existence, if by *proof* we mean a valid deduction of a conclusion from indubitable premises that all rational persons must accept. And the later presentations of his Reformed epistemology typically offered the following summary of the "Reformed attitude" to natural theology:

> A few Reformed thinkers—B. B. Warfield, for example—endorse the theistic proofs, but for the most part the Reformed attitude has ranged from tepid endorsement, through indifference, to suspicion, hostility, and outright accusations of blasphemy. (RBG, 63)

Indeed, Plantinga took Calvin's doctrine of the *sensus divinitatis* as an explanation of what he took to be a nearly universal consensus among the Reformed that the proofs were impious at worst, irrelevant at best. In support of "The Reformed Objection to Natural Theology," Plantinga cites Calvin and Bavinck to the effect that Christians don't need theistic proofs and ought not to base their belief on them (RBG, 67). Still, there seems to be a kind of plurality in both Plantinga and the Reformed tradition on this topic. Since Plantinga thinks that the classical standard of what counts as proof in natural theology is absurdly inflated, he is quite happy to reject that standard and endorse the cogency of literally dozens of simpler, intuitive arguments for God's existence from a broad range of starting points. And while he believes that the *sensus divinitatis* and the Holy Spirit can produce belief in God and the gospel (respectively) quite apart from argument, and ordinarily do so, Plantinga has no problem with theistic proofs having a kind of "intra-faith" application within the Christian community, serving to strengthen preexisting faith (TDOSTA, 461; NatT, 348). As for the Reformed tradition, there is B. B. Warfield, and more broadly a number of books have argued for a subtler relationship between the Reformed tradition and classical natural theology than Plantinga initially indicated.[8] It doesn't seem *essential* to the Reformed tradition to oppose classical natural theology, and anyone who doesn't share Plantinga's antipathy for such arguments can simply *add* them to Plantinga's repertoire.

Transcendental Argument

According to Reformed apologist Cornelius Van Til, classical natural theology is objectionable from a theological point of view, because such arguments accommodate the idea of neutrality, namely, that the existence of God should be settled by appeal to

8. A helpful examination of this issue is found in Michael Sudduth, *The Reformed Objection to Natural Theology* (New York: Routledge, 2009).

standards that are independent of the Christian worldview. In effect, they appeal to the autonomous standards of fallen man, overlooking the fact that God's revealed truth is the ultimate intellectual standard and possesses an authority that cannot be licensed, proved, or otherwise authorized by anything more ultimate than itself. Therefore, classical natural theology both conflicts with what the Bible says about its own authority and ignores what the Bible says about the fallen nature of man.

As an alternative, Van Til sets forth "transcendental argument" as a way of arguing for God's existence that is compatible with the Reformed tradition. On this view, the very possibility of knowledge and meaning, and of our access to them, depends on the truth of Christian theism, and it is the job of the Christian apologist to point this out. A transcendental argument doesn't start from neutral criteria, but from the presupposition of God's truth, and then shows that any views that deny God's truth end up denying the very possibility of knowledge and meaning. God *must* exist, because if he didn't, we couldn't know anything at all, much less reason or even make intelligible claims about the things we know.

It seems that transcendental argument, like supralapsarianism and the rejection of classical natural theology, is not a Reformed essential, even if it is widespread in the Reformed community due to Van Til's formidable influence. Still, many within the Reformed tradition are convinced that Van Til's analysis and alternative are correct. If so, how does Plantinga's own apologetic work measure up? On the one hand, Plantinga seems to share just as dim a view of the classical arguments as Van Til, though his reasons for this are epistemological rather than theological. As we saw above and in chapter 4, for Plantinga the classical arguments just don't work and simply aren't needed as a basis for faith.

On the other hand, many of Plantinga's apologetic arguments are similar to the transcendental argument, since they focus on the phenomena of epistemic self-defeat and self-referential incoherence.

In chapter 2, we saw Plantinga's argument that classical foundationalism about rationality is "self-referentially incoherent"; if it were true, we would have a good reason to reject it as false. In chapter 5, we saw Plantinga's argument that Grim's rejection of divine omniscience is self-defeating; if his conclusion is true, then his premises are false. We saw at the end of chapter 5 not only that the theological agnosticism of thinkers like Kant and John Hick is self-referentially incoherent, but also that any arguments for such views are self-defeating as well. In chapter 6, we saw Plantinga's argument that the fundamental assumptions of natural science seem to make the most sense when planted in Christian theological soil. "Given that we can have knowledge by way of science, what must be the case theologically?" is a central question for Plantinga. And at the end of chapter 6, we saw Plantinga's "naturalism defeated" argument, which says that if the naturalistic evolutionist's story were true, we'd have a good reason to think that we can't know anything at all. In all of this, we find Plantinga boldly criticizing the presuppositions and strategies of those opposed to the orthodox Christian faith, exposing them as self-defeating and destructive of the knowledge-seeking enterprise. This clearly seems to be much in the spirit of the Van Tilian apologetic project, even if it only loosely conforms to the letter of his principles. And, once again, the convinced Van Tilian can just *add* Van Til's style of argument to what is found in Plantinga; it's not like one blade on a Swiss army knife must exclude all the others.[9]

Classical Theism

There is currently (at time of writing) an ongoing reassessment of the extent to which the Reformed tradition presupposes

9. Relevant differences between Plantinga and Van Til in the area of apologetics are usefully compared in James Anderson, "If Knowledge Then God: The Epistemological Theistic Arguments of Plantinga and Van Til," *Calvin Theological Journal* 40, no. 1 (2005): 49–75.

or otherwise requires what has come to be known as "classical theism." The latter is generally taken to include formulations of the divine attributes widespread in the ancient and medieval period by authors such as the church fathers, Augustine, Anselm, and Aquinas. Key claims of classical theism are that God is metaphysically simple ("without parts"), timeless ("eternal"), absolutely unchanging ("immutable"), and without any passions ("without passions"). The fact that all of these quoted words are taken from the Westminster Confession of Faith, 2.1, is meant to indicate just some of the immense debt that the Reformed tradition has to classical theism.[10]

Simplicity

Where does Plantinga's body of work stand with respect to classical theism? Well, his rejection of the doctrine of divine simplicity in *Does God Have a Nature?* (1980) is pretty explicit, as we saw in chapter 5. So, any advocate of simplicity would have to reject Plantinga's line of thinking in that book as fundamentally mistaken (though he would still have to adequately face the challenges to that doctrine which Plantinga raises). There is no way around this.

Timelessness

On divine timelessness, Plantinga has curiously very little to say, except in two places. First, in *Does God Have a Nature?* he considers "Aquinas's doctrine of God's eternity or timelessness" and says that for Aquinas

> to add that he [God] is somehow timeless, somehow not in time at all, is to court a host of needless perplexities. There is nothing in Scripture or the essentials of the Christian message to support

10. See also the Belgic Confession, art. 1, which presents God as "simple," "eternal," and "unchangeable."

> this utterly opaque addition, and much that seems *prima facie* to militate against it. . . . God acts in time, acts at various times, and has done some things before he did others. It is at best Quixotic to deny this *prima facie* truth on the tenuous sorts of grounds alleged by those who do deny it. (*DGHAN*, 45–46)

Second, tucked away in a footnote in "Epistemic Probability and Evil," Plantinga says, "Here I assume (what seems to me to be true) that while God is indeed eternal, he is not timeless, 'outside of time' in the Boethian sense. (What I say can easily be restated to accommodate the latter view.)" (See EPAE, 94n11.)

Absolute Immutability

On divine immutability, again Plantinga doesn't have much to say, though he indirectly addresses the issue in his "Self-Profile," when he endorses the view that God suffers as God:

> As the Christian sees things, God does not stand idly by, coolly observing the suffering of his creatures. He enters into and shares our suffering. He endures the anguish of seeing his son, the second person of the Trinity, consigned to the bitterly cruel and shameful death of the cross. Some theologians claim that God cannot suffer. I believe they are wrong. God's capacity for suffering, I believe, is proportional to his greatness; it exceeds our capacity for suffering in the same measure as his capacity for knowledge exceeds ours. Christ was prepared to endure the agonies of hell itself; and God, the Lord of the universe, was prepared to endure the suffering consequent upon his son's humiliation and death. (SP, 36)

If in fact God suffers as God (and not just in the humanity of the Son), it is hard to see how he doesn't change in some respect, assuming he is not still suffering in this way now.

Without Passions

Finally, what about the classical denial of divine "passions"? In *Warranted Christian Belief*, Plantinga speaks of the affective side of conversion, which involves our loves, dispositions, and passions. Though he concedes that "here we may be crossing the boundary into groundless speculation," Plantinga finds an analogy to these in God himself, speaking of

> God's taking enormous pleasure, enjoyment, delight, happiness, delectation in the Son. Given the necessary existence of the Father and the Son, and their having their most important properties essentially, there is no way in which God could be deprived of the Son. . . . [footnote 44:] And this is the answer to one of the traditional arguments for the conclusion that God has no passions: the Father and the Son do indeed *need* each other, but it is a need that is necessarily and eternally fulfilled. (*WCB*, 320)

Let's say that Plantinga rejects all four claims of classical theism: God as simple, timeless, absolutely immutable, and without passions. How significant is this for the rest of Plantinga's philosophy? The answer seems to be: not much. As far as I can tell, no major Plantingian conclusion depends on his rejecting any of these elements of classical theism. Yes, Plantinga goes on record as making these moves. That cannot be denied. But he doesn't seem to *do* anything with them. It's not as if he denies simplicity or timelessness to come to some important conclusion elsewhere in his work. Presumably advocates of classical theism could just *replace* Plantinga's nonclassical theism with classical theism, without having to force much of a revision at all to the rest of Plantinga's published work. As Plantinga is quoted above, "What I say can easily be restated to accommodate the latter view" (e.g., timelessness).

Conclusion

Having completed this chapter's survey of Reformed themes and their relation to Plantinga, perhaps we should distinguish between not being Reformed and it *mattering* for Plantinga's philosophy or arguments whether or not he is Reformed. The former could be true, but the latter depends on the specific argument. As we've seen, by rejecting Plantinga's appeal to LFW and to Molinism, we lose a couple of his replies to the problem of evil. And approval of effectual calling, classical natural theology, Van Til's transcendental argument, and classical theism can just be *added* to Plantinga's positions, if one is so inclined. (I am so inclined!)

A lot of Plantinga's philosophy seems to be like this. He doesn't always avail himself of the distinctive Reformed theses and emphases that he *could* avail himself of. But it's not clear that he needs to do this in order for his arguments to do their job (such as rebut or undercut opponents' arguments or make a positive case for his own conclusions). We all fall short in various ways, but not all ways of falling short are created equal. To miss out on Reformed truth is regrettable, and the Reformed faith does in principle speak to everything, but it's not clear that the machinery of Plantinga's argumentation *always* depends on these truths. No doubt the International Space Station was built without those drawing up the relevant blueprints paying any substantial attention to the doctrine of the Trinity. It's not clear that the ISS is more prone to fail because of that!

In my view, Plantinga's body of work has made significant contributions to mature philosophical reflection on faith and reason, the problem of evil, theistic arguments, the divine attributes, religion and science, and the very method of Christian philosophy, while at the same time being strongly influenced by the Reformed tradition. In the providence of God, he has influenced a generation of Christian philosophers to be rigorous and bold in their defense of distinctive Christian claims. For my part, I'm grateful that so much good thinking has been made available to me to assess, build upon, and use discerningly. With all non-inspired authors, we rightly accept the dictum *caveat lector*. But as I consider the contemporary scene, with Plantinga I think it is also safe to add: *si monumentum requiris, circumspice* (if you seek his monument, look around).

GLOSSARY

antinomy. A pair of seemingly compelling arguments both for and against a claim. Kant appealed to antinomies to argue that we cannot know things in themselves (*noumena*), but only appearances (*phenomena*).

Aquinas/Calvin model. The claim that, in a wide variety of circumstances, the *sensus divinitatis* (when functioning properly) gives us true beliefs about, and therefore knowledge of, God.

autonomy (bad). Submitting not to God's law, but to oneself or to the world, as one's ultimate standard.

autonomy (good). Submitting not to oneself or to the world, but to God's law, as one's ultimate standard.

Christian apologetics. Using argument to defend and support Christian claims. The word *apologetics* comes from the Greek word *apologia,* meaning "a reasoned defense."

Christian philosophical criticism. Using philosophy to refute fundamental, worldview alternatives to Christian claims, while exposing the religious roots of such worldviews.

classical foundationalism. The view that for a belief to be rational, it must be self-evident, evident to the senses, or incorrigible (about one's inward mental state)—or ultimately based on beliefs like that.

classical theism. Formulations of the divine attributes widespread in the ancient and medieval period by authors such as the church fathers, Augustine, Anselm, and Aquinas. Key claims (which are also found in historic Protestant Reformed confessions) are that God is metaphysically simple (without parts), timeless (eternal), absolutely unchanging (immutable), and without any passions.

compatibilist free will. A kind of free will, said to be needed for moral responsibility, which is compatible with determinism. Usually this involves, at the very least, one's choices being uncoerced, responsive to reasons, and choices one would identify with. However, freedom to do otherwise in the same exact circumstances is not required.

constructive Christian philosophy. Answering traditional philosophical questions from the perspective of Christian claims. Examples: theistic theories of abstract objects, causality, natural laws, knowledge, mind, and probability. (Also called positive Christian philosophy.)

***de facto* question**. The question whether Christian belief is true or false.

***de jure* question**. The question whether Christian belief is warranted or not. Plantinga argues in *WCB* that any answer to the *de jure* question presupposes an answer to the *de facto* question. So the warrant for Christian belief depends on whether or not it is true, and cannot be determined independently of the latter consideration.

defense. A possible reason that God might have for permitting evil, which is used to show that God and evil are logically compatible. Plantinga offers a defense in his "free will defense."

divine simplicity. The doctrine that God has no parts whatsoever, whether these be spatial parts, temporal parts, or metaphysical parts. This is often aligned with the view that God is identical with his nature, that is, with his very attributes.

epistemology. The theory of knowledge, specifically of the sources, structure, analysis, and limits of knowledge.

evidentialist objection. The claim that theistic belief must be based on argument (that is, inferred from evidence) in order to be rational. This objection has often assumed classical foundationalism as the relevant standard of rationality.

evolution. According to Plantinga, a view of biological origins commonly associated with four theses: an ancient earth, progress of life from relatively simple to relatively complex forms, descent with modification, and common ancestry. Plantinga takes two further theses to be unscientific additions to evolution: naturalistic mechanism and naturalistic origins.

extended Aquinas/Calvin model. The claim that the work of the Holy Spirit in producing belief in "the great things of the gospel" is a kind of properly functioning process that satisfies the conditions of warrant. According to this model, Christian faith is a form of knowledge. This model therefore goes beyond what Plantinga says about the *sensus divinitatis* producing belief in God.

free will defense. An argument that God and evil are logically compatible because of the possibility that all possible free creatures suffer from "transworld depravity." This is a rebutting defeater for the problem of evil, showing that the claim that God and evil cannot coexist is false.

free will / foreknowledge dilemma. An argument that humans having libertarian free will is incompatible with God having infallible foreknowledge of how that freedom will be used.

Laplacean determinism. The view that the universe is physically determined and physically closed. It is associated with the eighteenth-century French mathematician and physicist Pierre Laplace.

libertarian free will. A kind of free will, said to be needed for moral responsibility, which is incompatible with determinism. Usually this is understood as the freedom to do otherwise in the same exact circumstances, such that no factor prior to your choice ensures that you make that choice.

maximal excellence. The property of being all-knowing, all-powerful, and perfectly good.

maximal greatness. The property of being maximally excellent in every possible world (that is, in every possible situation or every "way things could be").

metaphysics, compositional. The view that concrete properties are constituents or parts of the substances that have them.

metaphysics, relational. The view that abstract properties stand in a relation of "exemplification" to the concrete substances that exemplify the properties.

metaphysics. The theory of being, specifically of the fundamental categories of existing things and of how existing things relate at the most fundamental level. It includes theories of substance, properties, possibility, time, persistence, and causation.

Molinism. A view of providence, first propounded by the sixteenth-century Jesuit Luis de Molina, according to which God plans his universe by consulting truths about how free creatures would use their libertarian free will, if God were to create them and place them in various circumstances. These truths are available to God, for the purposes of his providential planning, prior to God making any choices as to what (if anything) shall exist.

natural theology. The discipline of offering arguments for God's existence from evidence that is available to all in the natural world, rather than from special verbal revelation (like the Bible). Examples: the cosmological argument (from the existence of the universe), the teleological argument (from apparent design), and the moral argument (from the phenomenon of conscience) for God's existence.

naturalism (metaphysical). The view that the space-time continuum is all there is, and that there are no supernatural beings such as God and angels.

ontological argument. An argument for the existence of God, first articulated by the medieval theologian Anselm of Canterbury, which seeks to prove from the mere fact that we have an idea of God that God must exist.

philosophical theology. The use of philosophy to explain or illuminate distinctive Christian claims (such as Trinity, incarnation, atonement, providence, inspiration, resurrection, and petitionary prayer).

philosophy of religion. Articulating and evaluating arguments for or against the coherence or truth of central religious claims.

pointless evil. According to atheist William Rowe, "instances of intense suffering which an omnipotent, omniscient being could have prevented without thereby losing some greater good or permitting some evil equally bad or worse." Such a being could "properly eliminate" such evils, and so (in Rowe's view) would eliminate them. So, their existence is evidence against God's existence. "Gratuitous evil" and "meaningless evil" are synonyms of "pointless evil."

power set theorem. The claim that the numerical size of a set is always less than the numerical size of the set of its subsets (its power set), from the nineteenth-century German mathematician Georg Cantor. Some have argued that this implies that there cannot be a set of all truths, and so there cannot be an omniscient being who knows all truths.

problem of evil. An argument against the existence of God which appeals to the existence of evil in the world. The "logical" problem says that evil makes God's existence impossible, whereas the "evidential" problem says that evil makes God's existence unlikely.

proper function. The way in which a cognitive faculty was designed to operate (either by God or evolution). Plantinga argues that this is an important element in any defensible theory of warrant.

properly eliminating an evil. Eliminating an evil without eliminating an outweighing good or bringing about a greater evil. (Otherwise, the elimination of the evil would be morally "improper.")

rationally permissible. Of a claim, when there is "nothing contrary to reason or irrational" in accepting it. We have no reason to think that such a claim is false or unlikely, and good reason to think it is possibly true.

rebutting defeater. A consideration which shows that an opponent's belief or conclusion is false.

Reformed epistemology. A response to the evidentialist objection to the rationality of belief in God. Reformed epistemology argues that (1) classical foundationalism is self-referentially incoherent and obviously false, and (2) belief in God can be properly basic and therefore rational if it is produced by the *sensus divinitatis*.

self-referential incoherence. Of a claim, if accepting it would give you a reason to reject it. Example: "there are no truths." If I were to accept this claim as true, I would thereby have reason to reject it as false.

sensus divinitatis. The idea, articulated in John Calvin's *Institutes of the Christian Religion*, that we have a God-given "sense of the divine," which supplies us with knowledge of God's existence, quite apart from any reliance on arguments for his existence.

skeptical theism. An undercutting defeater for the evidential problem of evil, which says that some evil may *appear* to be pointless, but we cannot reliably infer that it *is* in fact pointless. Only the latter would count as evidence against God's existence, not the former.

theodicy. According to Plantinga, a specific reason that would justify God in permitting evil. Plantinga offers a theodicy in SOFC.

transcendental argument. An argument that the very possibility of an experience, or the very possibility of the meaningfulness of a claim, depends upon something else that must be the case. A form of argument used by Immanuel Kant to deduce the ten "categories of the understanding," and adapted by Cornelius Van Til to argue for the existence of God.

transworld depravity. The condition of a possible free creature who would do at least one morally bad thing if created. In his free will defense, Plantinga appeals to the possibility that all possible free creatures suffer from transworld depravity.

undercutting defeater. A consideration which shows that an opponent's belief or conclusion is inadequately supported because it lacks reasons or grounds.

warrant. The property that any true belief must have if it is going to count as knowledge, and not just as a lucky guess. Philosophers differ as to whether warrant should be understood in terms of justification, rationality, proper function, or something else.

REFERENCES

References to Alvin Plantinga

In order not to burden the reader with laborious footnotes, listed here are all primary sources from Plantinga cited earlier in the book, alphabetized by title.

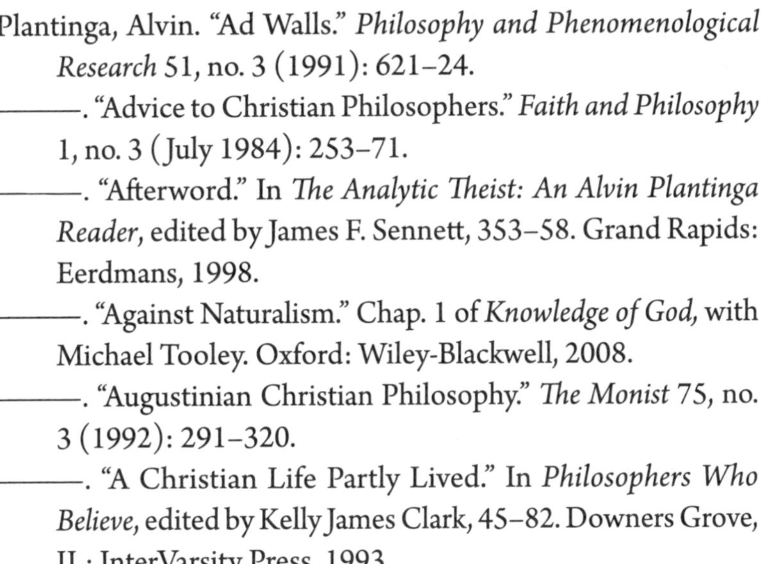

Plantinga, Alvin. "Ad Walls." *Philosophy and Phenomenological Research* 51, no. 3 (1991): 621–24.

———. "Advice to Christian Philosophers." *Faith and Philosophy* 1, no. 3 (July 1984): 253–71.

———. "Afterword." In *The Analytic Theist: An Alvin Plantinga Reader*, edited by James F. Sennett, 353–58. Grand Rapids: Eerdmans, 1998.

———. "Against Naturalism." Chap. 1 of *Knowledge of God*, with Michael Tooley. Oxford: Wiley-Blackwell, 2008.

———. "Augustinian Christian Philosophy." *The Monist* 75, no. 3 (1992): 291–320.

———. "A Christian Life Partly Lived." In *Philosophers Who Believe*, edited by Kelly James Clark, 45–82. Downers Grove, IL: InterVarsity Press, 1993.

———. "Christian Philosophy at the End of the 20th Century." In *Christian Philosophy at the Close of the Twentieth Century*, edited by Sander Griffioen and Bert Balk, 29–53. Kampen: Kok, 1995.

———. *Does God Have a Nature?* Milwaukee, WI: Marquette University Press, 1980.

———. "Epistemic Probability and Evil." *Archivio di filosofia* 56 (1988): 557–84. Reprinted in *Our Knowledge of God*, edited by Kelly James Clark, 39–63. Dordrecht: Kluwer, 1992. Also reprinted in *The Evidential Argument from Evil*, edited by Daniel Howard-Snyder, 69–96. Bloomington, IN: Indiana University Press, 1996. All citations refer to this reprint.

———. "An Evolutionary Argument against Naturalism." *Logos* 12 (1991): 27–49. Reprinted in *Faith in Theory and Practice: Essays on Justifying Religious Belief*, edited by Carol White and Elizabeth Radcliff, 35–65. Chicago: Open Court, 1993.

———. "The Evolutionary Argument against Naturalism." In *Naturalism Defeated? Essays on Plantinga's Evolutionary Argument against Naturalism*, edited by James Beilby, 1–12. Ithaca, NY: Cornell University Press, 2002.

———. "The Free Will Defense." In *Philosophy in America*, edited by Max Black, 204–20. Ithaca, NY: Cornell University Press, 1965.

———. *God and Other Minds*. Ithaca: Cornell University Press, 1967.

———. "God, arguments for the existence of." In *Routledge Encyclopedia of Philosophy*, edited by Edward Craig, pp. 85–93. London: Routledge, 1998.

———. *God, Freedom, and Evil*. New York: Harper Torchbook, 1974; Grand Rapids: Eerdmans, 1977.

———. "Is Belief in God Rational?" In *Rationality and Religious Belief*, edited by C. Delaney, 7–27. South Bend, IN: University of Notre Dame Press, 1979.

———. *Knowledge and Christian Belief*. New York: Oxford University Press, 2015.

———. "Law, Cause, and Occasionalism." In *Reason and Faith: Themes from Richard Swinburne*, edited by Michael Bergmann and Jeffrey E. Brower, 126–44. New York: Oxford University Press, 2016.

———. "Method in Christian Philosophy: A Reply." *Faith and Philosophy* 5, no. 2 (1988): 159–64.

———. "Natural Theology." In *A Companion to Metaphysics*, edited by Ernest Sosa and Jaegwon Kim, 346–49. Oxford: Blackwell, 1995.

———. *The Nature of Necessity*. New York: Oxford University Press, 1974.

———. "On Christian Scholarship." In *The Challenge and Promise of a Catholic University*, edited by Theodore Hesburgh. Notre Dame, IN: University of Notre Dame Press, 1994.

———. "On Ockham's Way Out." *Faith and Philosophy* 3, no. 3 (1986): 235–69.

———. "On Rejecting the Theory of Common Ancestry: A Reply to Hasker." *Perspectives on Science and Christian Faith* 44, no. 4 (December 1992): 258–63.

———. "The Probabilistic Argument from Evil." *Philosophical Studies* 35, no. 1 (1979): 1–53.

———. "The Prospects for Natural Theology." In *Philosophical Perspectives*, vol. 5, *Philosophy of Religion*, edited by James E. Tomberlin, 287–315. Atascadero, CA: Ridgeview Publishing Company, 1991.

———. "Reason and Belief in God." In *Faith and Rationality: Reason and Belief in God*, edited by Alvin Plantinga and Nicholas Wolterstorff, 16–93. Notre Dame, IN: University of Notre Dame Press, 1983.

———. "The Sceptics' Strategy." In *Faith and the Philosophers*, edited by John Hick, 226–27. London: St. Martin's Press, 1965.

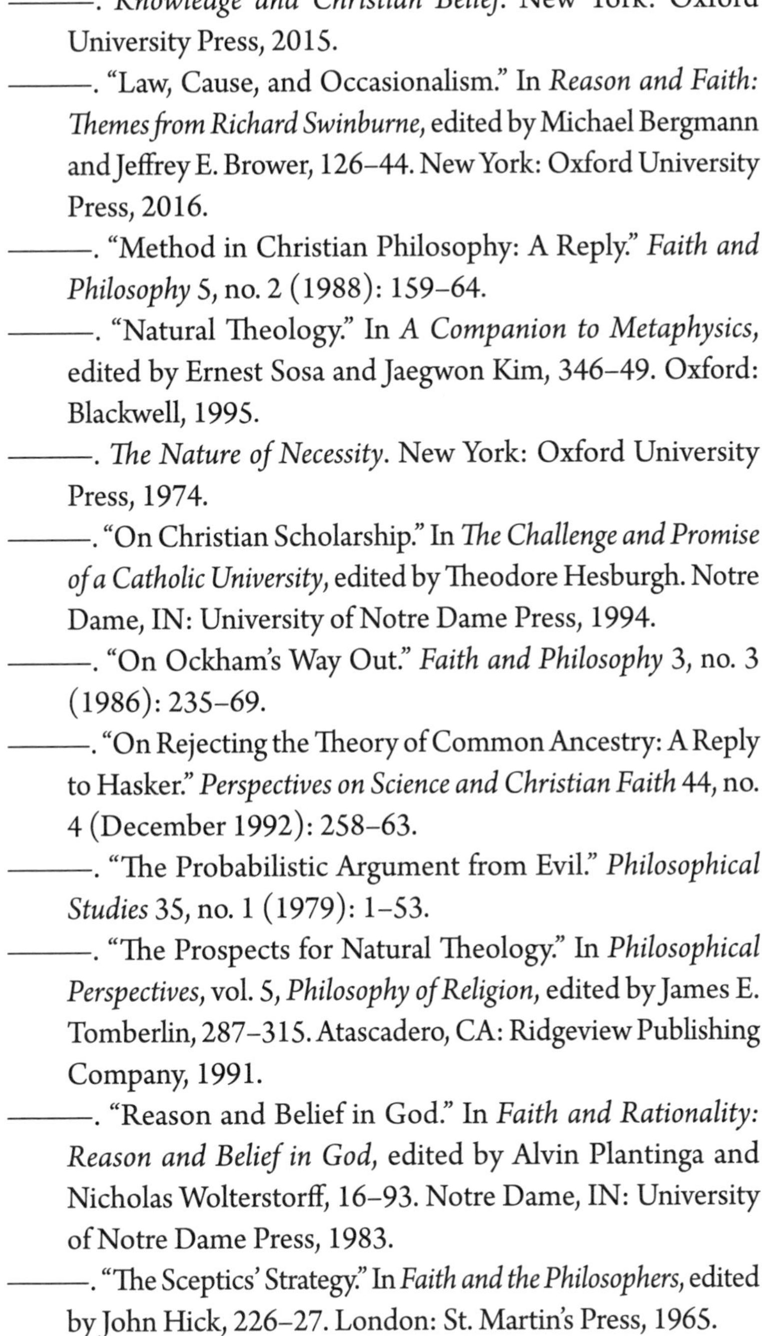

———. "Self-Profile." In *Alvin Plantinga,* edited by James Tomberlin and Peter van Inwagen, 3–97. Dordrecht: D. Reidel Publishing Company, 1985.

———. "Supralapsarianism, or 'O Felix Culpa.'" In *Christian Faith and the Problem of Evil,* edited by Peter van Inwagen, 1–25. Grand Rapids: Eerdmans, 2004. Reprinted in *The Problem of Evil: Selected Readings,* 2nd ed., edited by Michael Peterson, 363–89. Notre Dame, IN: University of Notre Dame Press, 2016. All citations are to this reprint.

———. "Truth, Omniscience, and Cantorian Arguments: An Exchange" (with Patrick Grim). *Philosophical Studies* 71, no. 3 (1993): 267–306.

———. "Two Dozen (or so) Theistic Arguments." In *Two Dozen (or so) Arguments for God: The Plantinga Project,* edited by Jerry Walls and Trent Dougherty, 461–79. New York: Oxford University Press, 2018.

———. *Warrant and Proper Function.* New York: Oxford University Press, 1993.

———. *Warrant: The Current Debate.* New York: Oxford University Press, 1993.

———. *Warranted Christian Belief.* New York: Oxford University Press, 2000. https://ccel.org/ccel/plantinga/warrant3.

———. *Where the Conflict Really Lies.* New York: Oxford University Press, 2011.

There are nearly two hundred books and papers written by Plantinga, and many of the most important ones are listed above. An incomplete, but very large online repository of papers by Plantinga is found at https://andrewmbailey.com/ap/.

References to Other Authors

Anderson, James. "If Knowledge Then God: The Epistemological Theistic Arguments of Plantinga and Van Til." *Calvin Theological Journal* 40, no. 1 (2005): 49–75.

Anderson, James N., and Paul Manata. "Determined to Come Most Freely: Some Challenges for Libertarian Calvinism." *Journal of Reformed Theology* 11, no. 3 (2017): 272–97.

Augustine. *City of God*. Translated by Henry Bettenson. New York: Penguin Books, 2003.

Bergmann, Michael, and Jeffrey E. Brower. "A Theistic Argument against Platonism (and in Support of Truthmakers and Divine Simplicity)." In *Oxford Studies in Metaphysics*, vol. 2, edited by Dean Zimmerman, 357–86. New York: Oxford University Press, 2006.

Brower, Jeffrey E. "Simplicity and Aseity." In *The Oxford Handbook of Philosophical Theology*, edited by Thomas Flint and Michael Rea, 105–28. New York: Oxford University Press, 2011.

Byerly, T. Ryan. "Free Will Theodicies for Theological Determinists." *Sophia* 56, no. 2 (2017): 289–310.

Hoitenga, Dewey. "Christian Theism: Ultimate Reality and Meaning in the Philosophy of Alvin Plantinga." *Ultimate Reality and Meaning* 23, no. 3 (September 2000): 211–37. https://doi.org/10.3138/uram.23.3.211.

Hume, David. *Dialogues concerning Natural Religion*. London, 1779.

Lewis, C. S. *The Problem of Pain*. New York: Macmillan, 1962.

Mackie, J. L. "Evil and Omnipotence." *Mind* 64, no. 254 (April 1955): 200–212.

Mackie, J. L. *The Miracle of Theism: Arguments for and against the Existence of God*. New York: Oxford University Press, 1982.

Rowe, William L. "The Problem of Evil and Some Varieties of Atheism." *American Philosophical Quarterly* 16, no. 4 (October 1979): 335–41.

Sudduth, Michael. *The Reformed Objection to Natural Theology.* New York: Routledge, 2009.

Walls, Jerry, and Trent Dougherty, eds. *Two Dozen (or so) Arguments for God: The Plantinga Project.* New York: Oxford University Press, 2018.

Welty, Greg. "Richard Swinburne: Pioneering Analytic Apologetics." In *The History of Apologetics: A Biographical and Methodological Introduction,* edited by Benjamin K. Forrest, Joshua D. Chatraw, and Alister E. McGrath, 714–33. Grand Rapids: Zondervan Academic, 2020.

Wykstra, Stephen J. "The Humean Objection to Evidential Arguments from Suffering: On Avoiding the Evils of 'Appearance.'" *International Journal for Philosophy of Religion* 16, no. 2 (1984): 73–93.

Zagzebski, Linda. "Foreknowledge and Free Will." In *The Stanford Encyclopedia of Philosophy,* edited by Edward N. Zalta. Fall 2004 edition. https://plato.stanford.edu/archives/fall2004/entries/free-will-foreknowledge/.

RECOMMENDED READING

If you read only three works by Alvin Plantinga, they should be *Knowledge and Christian Belief* (2015), *God, Freedom, and Evil* (1974), and "Advice to Christian Philosophers" (1984). These are shorter, more accessible expositions of Plantinga's views on epistemology, the ontological argument and the problem of evil, and philosophical method, which just happen to be the views for which he is most famous.

Many have examined various elements of Plantinga's thought. Their writings include the works listed below. Sources that are fairly accessible to non-philosophers are indicated by an asterisk.

Baker, Deane-Peter. *Tayloring Reformed Epistemology: Charles Taylor, Alvin Plantinga and the* de jure *Challenge to Christian Belief*. London: SCM Press, 2008.

Baker, Deane-Peter, ed. *Alvin Plantinga*. Cambridge: Cambridge University Press, 2007.

*Baldwin, Erik, and Tyler Dalton McNabb. *Plantingian Religious Epistemology and World Religions: Prospects and Problems*. Studies in Comparative Philosophy and Religion. Lanham, MD: Lexington Books, 2019.

*Beilby, James. *Epistemology as Theology: An Evaluation of Alvin Plantinga's Religious Epistemology*. Farnham, UK: Ashgate, 2006.

Beilby, James, ed. *Naturalism Defeated? Essays on Plantinga's Evolutionary Argument against Naturalism*. Ithaca, NY: Cornell University Press, 2002.

*Clark, Kelly James. *Return to Reason*. Grand Rapids: Eerdmans, 1990.

Clark, Kelly James, and Michael Rea, eds. *Reason, Metaphysics, and Mind: New Essays on the Philosophy of Alvin Plantinga*. New York: Oxford University Press, 2012.

*Diller, Kevin. *Theology's Epistemological Dilemma: How Karl Barth and Alvin Plantinga Provide a Unified Response*. Downers Grove, IL: IVP Academic, 2014.

*Hoitenga, Dewey. "Christian Theism: Ultimate Reality and Meaning in the Philosophy of Alvin Plantinga." *Ultimate Reality and Meaning* 23, no. 3 (September 2000): 211–37. https://doi.org/10.3138/uram.23.3.211.

*Hoitenga, Dewey. *From Plato to Plantinga: An Introduction to Reformed Epistemology*. Albany: State University of New York Press, 1991.

Kim, Joseph. *Reformed Epistemology and the Problem of Religious Diversity*. Eugene, OR: Pickwick Publications, 2011.

Kvanvig, Jonathan L., ed. *Warrant in Contemporary Epistemology: Essays in Honor of Plantinga's Theory of Knowledge*. Lanham, MD: Rowman & Littlefield, 1996.

*Mascord, Keith. *Alvin Plantinga and Christian Apologetics*. Milton Keynes, UK: Paternoster, 2006.

Slagle, Jim. *The Evolutionary Argument against Naturalism: Context, Exposition, and Ramifications*. New York: Bloomsbury Academic, 2021.

Tomberlin, James, and Peter van Inwagen, eds. *Alvin Plantinga*. Dordrecht: D. Reidel Publishing Company, 1985.

Zagzebski, Linda, ed. *Rational Faith: Catholic Responses to Reformed Epistemology*. Notre Dame, IN: Notre Dame University Press, 1993.

INDEX OF SUBJECTS AND NAMES

Greg Welty (DPhil, University of Oxford) is professor of philosophy at Southeastern Baptist Theological Seminary in Wake Forest, North Carolina (2010–present). He has been married to his wife, Rose, for twenty-six years, and they have three sons. He was born and raised in Los Angeles, California, and is a graduate of the University of California, Los Angeles (BA, philosophy), Westminster Theological Seminary in California (MDiv), and the University of Oxford (MPhil, DPhil, philosophical theology; Oriel College, supervisor: Richard Swinburne). He was a teaching assistant for John Frame at Westminster (1993–1997), a stipendiary lecturer in philosophy at Regent's Park College, University of Oxford (2000–2001), and an assistant professor of philosophy at Southwestern Baptist Theological Seminary in Ft. Worth, Texas (2003–2010).

He is also the program coordinator for the MA in philosophy of religion at Southeastern, and served as a pastor for over ten years. He specializes in the relation between abstract objects and God, the problem of evil, theories of divine providence, theistic arguments, and philosophy of religion more generally. He is the author, most recently, of *Why Is There Evil in the World?* (Christian Focus, 2018), is coeditor of *Calvinism and Middle Knowledge: A Conversation* (Pickwick Publications, 2019), and coedits *The Big Ten—Critical Questions Answered* (Christian Focus, 2016–), a series of ten apologetics volumes. He has contributed to *Contemporary Arguments in Natural Theology: God and Rational Belief* (Bloomsbury Academic, 2021), *The History of Apologetics: A Biographical and Methodological Introduction* (Zondervan Academic, 2020), *Philosophical Essays against Open Theism* (Routledge, 2018), *Calvinism and the Problem of Evil* (Pickwick Publications, 2016), *Beyond the Control of God? Six Views on the Problem of God and Abstract Objects* (Bloomsbury Academic, 2014), and *Calvinism: A Southern Baptist Dialogue* (B&H Academic, 2008). He has also contributed to *Philosophia Christi, Faith and Philosophy, Themelios,* and the Concise Theology project at The Gospel Coalition, and has served as a referee for several journals in philosophy of religion.

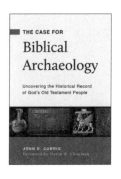

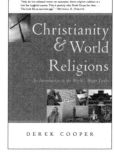

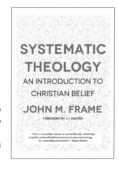

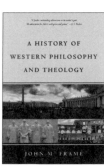

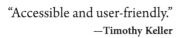

ALSO FROM P&R PUBLISHING

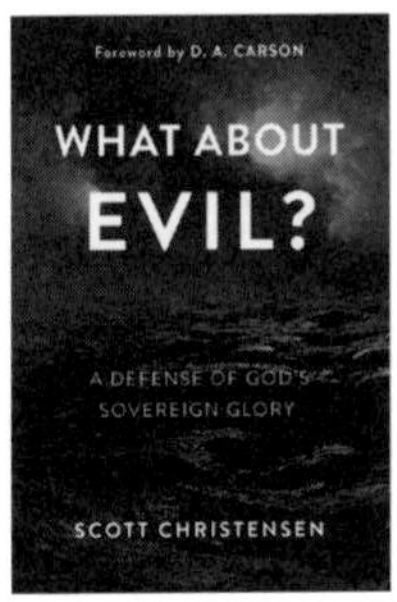

Reconciling the existence of God and evil is a conundrum in Christian theology, and a philosophical approach—rather than a theological one—dominates. Turning to the Bible's grand storyline, Scott Christensen examines how sin, evil, corruption, and death fit into the broad outlines of redemptive history. He argues that God's ultimate end in creation is to magnify his glory to his image bearers, most notably by defeating evil through the atoning work of Christ.

"Christensen's interaction with contemporary literature on this topic is both wide-ranging and charitable, and much profit may be gained in considering how he lays out his case. . . . Highly recommended."
—**Greg Welty**, Professor of Philosophy, Southeastern Baptist Theological Seminary; author, *Why Is There Evil in the World?*

"Christensen . . . remind[s] us that God's wisdom pervades everything he ordains so that the very existence of evil serves his purpose of maximizing goodness and glorifying himself. Of course, Romans 8:28 and other verses *say* that this is true. But Christensen shows us *how* it is true, how even in this fallen world we can begin to grasp something of God's light in the midst of the darkness, indeed *especially* there. I commend this book to readers who seek a serious and thoughtful treatment of this issue."
—**John M. Frame**, Professor of Systematic Theology and Philosophy Emeritus, Reformed Theological Seminary, Orlando

Was this book helpful to you?
Consider writing a review online.
The author appreciates your feedback!

Or write to P&R at editorial@prpbooks.com
with your comments. We'd love to hear from you.